STUDY GUIDE FOR

WORLD HISTORY

VOLUME I: TO 1800

PREPARED BY
DIANNA RHYAN KARDULIAS
COLUMBUS STATE COMMUNITY COLLEGE

West/Wadsworth
I(T)P® An International Thomson Publishing Company

Belmont, CA • Albany, NY • Bonn • Boston • Cincinnati • Detroit • Johannesburg • London
Madrid • Melbourne • Mexico City • New York • Paris • Singapore • Tokyo • Toronto • Washington

Printed in the United States of America
1 2 3 4 5 6 7 8 9 10

For more information, contact Wadsworth Publishing Company, 10 Davis Drive, Belmont, CA 94002, or electronically at http://www.thomson.com/wadsworth.html

International Thomson Publishing Europe
Berkshire House 168-173
High Holborn
London, WC1V 7AA, England

International Thomson Editores
Campos Eliseos 385, Piso 7
Col. Polanco
11560 México D.F. México

Thomas Nelson Australia
102 Dodds Street
South Melbourne 3205
Victoria, Australia

International Thomson Publishing Asia
221 Henderson Road
#05-10 Henderson Building
Singapore 0315

Nelson Canada
1120 Birchmount Road
Scarborough, Ontario
Canada M1K 5G4

International Thomson Publishing Japan
Hirakawacho Kyowa Building, 3F
2-2-1 Hirakawacho
Chiyoda-ku, Tokyo 102, Japan

International Thomson Publishing GmbH
Königswinterer Strasse 418
53227 Bonn, Germany

International Thomson Publishing Southern Africa
Building 18, Constantia Park
240 Old Pretoria Road
Halfway House, 1685 South Africa

ISBN 0-534-53128-8

Table Of Contents

How to Use This Study Guide

I. Outlining the Chapter

Previewing this list makes you aware of the chapter's structure before you even begin. As you read, refer back to this outline in order to remain aware of where you are on this "reading map." It reflects not only the order in which topics will be presented, but also their relative importance within this emerging network of ideas.

Treat the Conclusion as a chapter summary: be sure you understand the details of the large movements and changes outlined in these last few paragraphs.

II. Terms and Persons To Know

These are listed in order of presentation. Taken together, these present a summary of the chapter's ideas. Read the chapter with this list beside you and always pause when you come across a term. Collect information from the surrounding paragraphs, take notes for each item, and make sure you understand each one before you move on. This section is especially helpful in preparation for multiple choice, true/false, or fill-in-the-blank tests your professor might give in the future, because these terms and persons are likely to be among those targeted. This section also is a tremendous help in preparing for essay exams, where a *detailed* answer, i.e., an answer which demonstrates specific knowledge of persons and terms, is superior to a general (or vague) answer.

III. Mapwork

IV. Datework

V. Primary Sourcework

VI. Artwork

Sections III-VI present you with some of the materials that scholars have consulted in order to form their ideas and thus to create the narrative content of each chapter. Such documents and art are primary sources. The maps, timelines, and chronologies serve to orient you on the globe and to specific historical points in time. Each of these supplementary features engages your mind in a different way, and the questions in this study guide that accompany them invite you to think critically about what each feature means. This is altogether different from just looking at them for a moment and then moving on. These brief queries are designed to deepen your understanding of what the main text of each chapter is about. For example, the text of Chapter One describes the Assyrian army. But don't stop there. There are primary sources (original documents from Assyrian kings themselves, and from Old Testament writers who mention Assyrian military might) included as excerpts to bring the text alive. There is a map of the Assyrian empire. There is a table of Semitic languages (one of which the Assyrians spoke), there are examples of Assyrian art demonstrating their weapons, soldiers, and some consequences of their campaigns, and there are timelines that show the development of Assyrian culture and what else was happening in the world at that time. These ancillary materials help to fix the chapter's main text in your memory, and give you vivid details the text can't include. In addition, using these sections encourages you to learn this material in an active rather than a passive mode. After you read the chapter, set aside time to study the maps, timelines and chronologies, primary sources, and art.

VII. Identifying Important Concepts Behind the Conclusion

The Conclusion to each chapter consists of a few paragraphs that serve to recall that chapter's most important ideas to your mind, to summarize them, and to reinforce them. This means that each major idea receives just a few concise sentences. Use the Conclusion as a memory refresher, and view it as a handy chapter summary.

Later, after your initial reading, when you turn back to review a chapter, it can be to your advantage to *begin* with this section (and then end with it too).

Example: The Key Ideas from the Conclusion to Chapter One

1. rise of civilization

2. first great civilizations: Mesopotamia and Egypt

3. Hebrew monotheism

4. next great empires: Assyria and Persia

The idea is not to be too detailed here, but to encourage yourself at this final stage to think in the broadest terms. The ability to synthesize and to summarize now readies you to do precisely that on essay questions your professor might assign in the future. If you want to review details, you can always turn back to **Section II: Terms and Persons to Know**. In fact, one good way to study the Conclusion is to refer back to these terms and persons for a new reason: in order to note which terms and persons belong under which main ideas in the Conclusion. For example, the person "Hammurabi" from Section II belongs to the second main idea in our conclusion outline, i.e. to the first great civilization of Mesopotamia; the term "Neolithic Revolution," however, belongs to the first main idea, i.e. to the rise of civilization. By taking these steps, you make sure that you have mentally organized this chapter's most important general concepts before moving on to the next chapter.

P.S. How many times should you read a chapter? (Notice that it is assumed that you will read it more than once.) At least twice, and as many times as you need to in order to fully absorb its contents. Read through the first time in order to complete **Section II**. Then page through, pausing to think critically (guided by the questions here) about each timeline, primary source, artwork, and table, making sure you see how each piece of evidence fits into the chapter's structure of ideas. Finally, understand that you most definitely will need to put more effort into Chapter One than into, say, Chapter Twelve; this is because you are going to get better at studying for this course. In other words, this study guide is not only preparing you for class discussion and exams, but is designed to develop your reading, comprehension, organization, and critical thinking skills. They will develop if you faithfully use the guide; this will most likely result in a smoother learning process for later chapters than earlier ones. You will be processing and organizing the information at a higher level of competence.

Chapter One
The First Civilizations: The Peoples of Western Asia and Egypt

I. Outlining the Chapter

The First Humans
- Hunter-Gatherers of the Stone Age
- Agricultural Revolution, c. 10,000-4,000 B.C.E.

Emergence of Civilization

Civilization in Mesopotamia
- City-States of Ancient Mesopotamia
- Empires in Ancient Mesopotamia
  - Code of Hammurabi

Culture of Mesopotamia
  - Importance of Religion
  - Cultivation of New Arts and Sciences

Egyptian Civilization: "The Gift of the Nile"
- Old and Middle Kingdoms
- Society and Economy in Ancient Egypt
- Culture of Egypt
  - Spiritual Life in Egyptian Society
  - Pyramids
  - Art and Writing
- Chaos and a New Order: The New Kingdom
- Daily Life in Ancient Egypt: Family and Marriage

New Centers of Civilization
- Impact of the Indo-Europeans
- Phoenicians
- Hebrews: The "Children of Israel"
  - Spiritual Dimensions of Israel
  - Uniqueness of the Hebrew Religion

The Rise of New Empires
- Assyrian Empire
  - Assyrian Society and Culture
- Persian Empire
  - Governing the Empire
  - Persian Religion

Conclusion

II. Terms and Persons To Know

hominids

Homo sapiens sapiens

Paleolithic peoples

Neolithic revolution

Çatal Hüyük

Neolithic Age living and labor patterns

writing

metals: copper, bronze, iron

Civilization: definition

Mesopotamia

Sumerians

Akkadians

Sargon

Amorites (Old Babylonians)

Hammurabi

Code of Hammurabi

polytheism

divination

cuneiform writing

Gilgamesh

Nile

dynasties

Old Kingdom

Intermediate periods

Menes

pharaoh

ma'at

bureaucracy

vizier

nomarch

Middle Kingdom

social hierarchy of Egypt

sun cult

Osiris cult

Book of the Dead

pyramids

art: function and canon

ka

hieroglyphs

Hyksos

New Kingdom

Amenhotep IV or Akhenaten

Ramses II

wisdom literature

marriage

Neolithic Europe

Stonehenge

Indo-Europeans

Hittites

Phoenecians

Hebrews

Judaism

Hebrew Bible

Exodus

Solomon

Israel and Judah

monotheism

YHWH

covenant

law

prophets

Assyrian Empire

Ashurbanipal

Assyrian military monarchy

Nebuchadnezzar II

Persians

Cyrus the Great

Darius

satrapies

Great Kings

Zoroastrianism

Ahuramazda

ethical dualism

III. Mapwork

Map 1.1. Spread of *Homo sapiens sapiens*

Where did our species originate?

What patterns of living led us to travel far from our original sites of habitation?

Map 1.2. Development of Agriculture

Why do the first civilizations originate in river valleys?

Which crops are produced by early agricultural societies? How does this differ from the diet of earlier paleolithic peoples?

What developments in human society does agriculture initiate?

Map 1.3. Ancient Mesopotamia

Which modern country exists today where once stood Çatal Hüyük? Jericho?

Which modern countries occupy the region once known as Mesopotamia?

Identify the two rivers that gave Mesopotamia its name.

Identify the five independent city-states of Sumer.

Why has this region traditionally been called "the fertile crescent"? What geographical features border this region to the north? south? east? southwest?

Map 1.4. Ancient Egypt

How much of Egypt is arable land? Why?

How did the cataracts on the Nile affect Egyptian contact with lands to the south?

What danger does the Mediterranean Sea represent to the Egyptian empire, particularly from the end of the New Kingdom to the time of Cleopatra?

Identify the capital cities of: the Old Kingdom, the New Kingdom, and Akhenaten.

Which city was of primary importance to the priests of Amon-Re?

Which of the Egyptian Kingdoms is makes Giza a site of superior monumental architecture? Which is known for adorning Karnak and Luxor?

Map 1.5. Ancient Palestine

How far away from ancient Palestine were the regions of ancient Mesopotamia and Egypt?

Which of the cities in this region was the site of Solomon's temple?

What affect did the Assyrian empire have on the kingdom of Israel? Why was Israel, more than Judah, more vulnerable to the Assyrian military machine?

How did geography play a crucial role in causing the Phoenecians to become known as important traders and transmitters of language?

Map 1.6. Assyrian and Persian Empires

In what ways did the Royal Road serve the purposes of the Great Kings of Persia?

Identify the capital cities of the following: the Assyrian empire, Nebuchadnezzar II, the Achaemenid dynasty, the Persian empire. Considering the last city, however, where did Darius prefer to live?

How did the Persian empire change between 557 and 539 B.C.E.?

Did the Persian empire ever gain control of India (to the east) or Greece (to the west)?

IV. Datework

Timeline for Part I: The development of agriculture and neolithic towns to the Roman empire expanding into the Middle East

Why does this timeline begin at 6,000 B.C.E.? Why not in 10,000 B.C.E.?

Where are the first five agricultural-based civilizations located? Do events in these five regions run closely parallel, or do they differ? Why?

What empire has gained control of the Middle East and Egypt by the year zero?

What is meant by the terms B.C.E. and C.E.? (The change, which comes at the end of this timeline, is explained in the preface to the textbook.) What terms do they replace? Why is the change in terminology significant?

Locate these cultures by order of appearance and by geographical location: Sumerian, Harappan, Han, Minoan.

Chapter Timeline: The emergence of city-states to the height of Persian power

On the bottom band of this timeline, note the following features, listed in chronological order: Great Pyramid, Code of Hammurabi, Age of Zoroastrianism, and Prophets in Israel. Assign each of these to its approximate date and to its proper culture.

Which of the Mesopotamian empires is powerful during the time of the Egyptian Old Kingdom? Middle Kingdom? New Kingdom? What follows?

Chronology: The First Humans

Were Australopithecines hominids?

What were the differences between Neanderthals and *Homo sapiens sapiens*? Did these two species overlap? Did they interact?

What was *Homo erectus* the first to do?

Chronology: Chief Events in Mesopotamian History

How do Sargon, Ur-Nammu, and Hammurabi each shape Mesopotamian history after the initial development of the Sumerian city-states?

Chronology: Egyptians

How does the third-century B.C.E. Egyptian scholar Manetho still influence our organization of Egyptian history today?

What distinguishes a "Kindom" from an "Intermediate Period"?

Why is the period after 1085 B.C.E. termed "Post-Empire"?

Why does this chronology begin in 3100 B.C.E.? Why does it end in 30 B.C.E.?

Chronology: Hebrews

What is the significance of the Exodus from Egypt in Hebrew history? Is this event remembered as important in Egyptian history? Why or why not?

Where would Moses be placed in this chronology? The prophets?

Which event on this chronology is commemorated in Psalm 137?

Chronology: The Empires (Assyria and Persia)

What factors bring about the destruction of the Assyrian empire?

What differences characterize the kingships of the Assyrian Ashurbanipal and the Persian Cyrus the Great?

What were the achievements of Cambyses and Darius?

V. Primary Sourcework

Mesopotamian Primary Sources:

Code of Hammurabi

Why did Hammurabi's law code emphasize the principle of retribution?

What evidence do you see here for differential treatment according to social status?

What seems to be the role of females? What purpose did marriage serve? How do your answers differ from the answers you might give if you were studying current U.S. laws?

The Great Flood (from the *Epic of Gilgamesh*)

The Old Testament story of Noah is narrated in the third person; in the *Epic of Gilgamesh*, Utnapishtim appears to the hero Gilgamesh and tells his own story. Does the account affect you differently as a result?

Why do the gods decide to destroy humankind according to the Mesopotamian version? How does this reflect Mesopotamian polytheism and Hebrew ethical monotheism?

Egyptian Primary Sources:

Hymn to the Nile and Hymn to the Pharaoh

Why is the life-giving river Nile personified in this Hymn? What, according to this hymn, would Egypt lack if the Nile were to disappear?

Why was the pharaoh said to "unite the Two Lands?"

What would Egypt lack if the pharaoh were to disappear? How does this relate to Egyptian belief in the pharaoh's role in the maintenance of *ma'at*?

Chronologically speaking, to which Egyptian Kingdom would Seostris III have belonged? Which two dynasties flourished then?

Akhenaten's Hymn to Aton

Why is Amenhotep IV more commonly known as Akhenaten?

After his death, some of Akhenaten's successors referred to him as "the criminal" or "the rebel king." Why did this happen? How does this hymn document his "rebellion"?

What relation to the god Aten is the pharaoh claiming here?

Hebrew Primary Sources:

Exodus 19: 1-8

Where is the desert of Sinai on the possible exodus route? (See map 1.5.)

What relationship does the covenant establish between God and the Israelites?

What are the ten commandments?

Do you see any similarities between these commandments and the law code of Hammurabi?

Isaiah 3: 14-17, 24-26 and Amos 3: 1-2

According to Isaiah, why did God punish the Hebrew people? How does this differ from the reason Amos gives?

What punishments did the Hebrews suffer?

Why is the Assyrian called "the rod of my anger?" What historical event is being alluded to here?

Assyrian Primary Sources:

Assyrian Kings' Writings: King Sennacherib Describes a Battle with the Elamites and His Siege of Jerusalem, and King Ashurbanipal Describes His Treatment of Conquered Babylon

Why did Assyrian kings promulgate writings of this kind?

Why do Sennacherib and Ashurbanipal prefer to say "I" rather than "We" (thus including his generals and soldiers) in these documents?

What has happened to the Chaldeans who opposed Sennacherib? What about the Israelites who opposed him? According to these documents, what military tactics have been employed in these campaigns?

VI. Artwork

Prehistoric Art:

Paleolithic Cave Painting

What purposes might paintings of this kind have served?

What subjects are commonly depicted in Paleolithic cave paintings? What human concerns are expressed in this type of art?

Humans are very rarely depicted in Paleolithic art. Why do you think this is so?

Mesopotamian Art:

"Royal Standard" of Ur

Where is Ur on the map of Mesopotamia? (See map 1.3)

How has the artist distinguished the Sumerian king from his nobles and his subjects?

What statement do the luxury goods and leisure activities represented here make about the kings of the Sumerian city-states?

Could the king depicted here be Hammurabi? Why not?

Stele of Hammurabi (Code of Hammurabi, King of Babylonia)

Among all the gods worshipped in Babylonia, why is Shamash, the god of justice, depicted on this stele?

Why did Hammurabi order such stelai to be placed throughout his empire?

Although some similarities in dress between Hammurabi and Shamash are evident, how has the artist distinguished the god from the king? Although the two figures' heads occupy the same level on the stele, are the two figures really the same height? How has the artist achieved this deceptive effect and for what purpose?

What gesture is Shamash making? What gesture is Hammurabi making in return? Which portion of the stele had greatest meaning for the majority of Babylonians, the picture or the cuneiform nscription below? Why?

Egyptian Art:

Pair Statue of King Menkaure and His Queen

Chronologically speaking, to which of the Egyptian Kingdoms did Menkaure and his queen belong?

What evidence is presented here for the status of Great Wife in the pharaoh's household? Is the queen depicted as subordinate to her husband in any way?

How does this sculpture idealize the king and queen? Is this a portrait of the pharaoh, an image of him as god and divine instrument, or a combination of the two?

Great Pyramid of Giza

Chronologically speaking, which dynasties ruled Egypt during the period when the pyramids were built?

Where is Giza? With which Old Kingdom city was it associated? (See map 1.4.)

How were the pyramids designed to serve the pharaoh's *ka*?

Could anyone in Egypt cause a pyramid to be built except the pharaoh (and his immediate family)? Why not?

Egyptian Hunting Scene

How do we know that this painting depicts members of the Egyptian upper classes? Why are the figures in the lower portions of the artwork depicted as relatively small? Who do you think they are?

What evidence do you see here for the canonical principles underlying Egyptian art? Is this restricted to the human figures, or has it also determined the representation of vegatative and animal forms?

Locate the hieroglyphic writing in this painting. What evidence do you see of its probable pictorial origins?

Neolithic European Art:

Stonehenge

What does Stonehenge indicate about Neolithic European culture?

Where have megaliths been found?

Assyrian Art:

The King of Israel Pays Tribute to the King of Assyria

How are the King of Israel and the King of Assyria distinguished from each other on this obelisk? Why?

Consider this artwork again in light of the primary source readings "The Hebrew Prophets: Isaiah and Amos" and "The Assyrian Military Machine." Does this scene reinforce or refute what the documents say about the interaction of Israel and Assyria?

King Ashurbanipal's Lion Hunt

Why does some of the richest Assyrian art in the world come from archaeological sites at the location of ancient Nineveh?

Is King Ashurbanipal in any danger here? Does he seem to mind? What statement is being made about Assyrian kingship?

Archers of the Persian Guard

To whom would this famous infantry force have appeared "immortal," to the Persians or to their enemies? Why? What made this appearance an effective military tactic?

This frieze originally adorned the palace of a Persian Great King. Why would it be effective decoration for his residence?

We have seen that ancient Egyptian art was more idealizing than realistic. What evidence do you see that Persian art had some of the same tendencies?

VIa. Tablework

Semitic Languages

What two Semitic languages are still spoken today? How do scholars know that the others ever existed?

What similarities do you see between the names of the languages in this linguistic family and the history of empires in Mesopotamia?

Cuneiform Writing

Why would a system of writing, such as cuneiform, become less and less pictorial over time?

What writing instrument gave cuneiform writing its characteristic shape?

Who invented cuneiform? What advantages does such a writing system give to its civilization?

Which of the primary source documents in this chapter would have first been written down in cuneiform writing?

How did the Egyptians use pictographs? How did the Phoenecians later simplify writing?

Some Indo-European Languages

Who were the Indo-Europeans? How did they come to be called this?

Were the Semitic languages or the Indo-European languages ancestral to most European languages spoken today? Were any Indo-European languages important in the Mesopotamian world?

VII. Identifying Important Concepts Behind the Conclusion

The Conclusion to Chapter One recalls the following key ideas:

1. rise of civilization (i.e., the skills and inventions of humans prior to civilization, followed by the achievements of humans within the first city-states)

2. first civilizations: Mesopotamia and Egypt

3. Hebrew legacy of monotheism

4. next great civilizations: Assyria and Persia

For more information, see the introduction to Part I: "The First Civilizations and Rise of Empires." Review these general concepts before moving on to Chapter Two.

Chapter Two: Ancient India

I. Outlining the Chapter

Background to the Emergence of Civilization in India

Harappan Civilization: A Fascinating Enigma
- Political and Social Structures
- Harappan Culture

Arrival of the Aryans
- Art of Statecraft in Ancient India: The *Arthasastra*
- Caste and Class: Social Structures in Ancient India
  - Caste System
  - Daily Life in Ancient India
  - Economy

Escaping the Wheel of Life: The Religious World of Ancient India
- Hinduism
  - Reincarnation
- Buddhism: The Middle Path
  - Asoka, A Buddhist Monarch

Rule of the Fishes: India after the Mauryas

Exuberant World of Indian Culture
- Literature
- Architecture and Sculpture

Conclusion

II. Terms and Persons To Know

Ganges River

Indus River valley

Dravidians

Aryans

Harappan civilization

Mohenjo-Daro

clay seals

Alexander the Great

Chandragupta Maurya

14

Mauryan empire

Arthasastra

raja

kshatriya

maharaja

dharma

brahmin

caste system

varna

vaisyas

sudras

jati

importance of family

importance of males

monsoon

Hinduism

Vedas

sacrifice

asceticism

Upanishads

Brahman

reincarnation

karma

Buddhism

Siddhartha Gautama

nirvana

Middle Path

Jainism

Asoka

Kushan Kingdom

Sanskrit

Mahabharata

Ramayana

pillar

stupa

rock chamber

III. Mapwork

Map 2.1. Ancient Harappan Civilization

How was the geographical site of Harappan civilization similar to that of Sumer?

Locate the following features on the map: Indus river, Ganges river, Himalayan mountains.

Look to the east: how far away were the cultures of Mesopotamia?

Map 2.2. The Citadel at Mohenjo Daro

What features indicate how the assembly hall, granary, college, and bath were to be defended?

Why would the community's granary be located within the citadel? Why near the stair?

What are the unmarked, small, connected chambers on this plan?

Map 2.3. The Empire of Asoka

What was the purpose of Asoka's pillar and rock edicts? What pattern do you discern in their placement?

What happened to the Mauryan empire after Asoka's death?

IV. Datework

Chapter Timeline: First Indian agricultural settlements to the Reign of Asoka

Was Harappan civilization contemporaneous with Sumerian civilization?

When do the Aryans arrive? From where?

How long ago had Gautama Buddha lived when Asoka began to spread Buddhism?

Chronology: Ancient India

Do the Aryans bring an end to Harappan civilization?

For how long is the Mauryan dynasty an important centralizing force in India? How does the collapse of the Mauryan dynasty lead to the rise of the Kushan Kingdom?

What effect does does Gautama Buddha have on Hinduism, the religious legacy of the Aryans?

V. Primary Sourcework

Hindu Primary Sources:

Bits of Wisdom from Ancient India: The Mahabharata

Who was the intended audience of the Mahabharata?

What is the significance of *dharma* in Hinduism? In Buddhism, does this remain an important concept?

What evidence do you see here for an Aryan concern with the Self?

The Duties of a King: The *Arthasastra*

At whose court did Kautilya apparently live?

What similarities do you perceive between this passage and the excerpt from the Bhagavadgita that introduced this chapter? How did these two literary works differ in purpose?

Social Classes in Ancient India: The *Law of Manu*

How many castes are described in this treatise? What are their respective functions?

What was the original Indian word for class (or caste)? What was its original meaning?

Who is "the Self-Existent One"?

What evidence does this document provide for the Hindu concern with sacrifice? With reincarnation?

What defines a "twice-born person" (mentioned in the final paragraph)?

The Position of Women in Ancient India: The *Law of Manu*

What features in this passage allow it justly to be described as "ambivalent" toward women?

What evidence do you see here for the supremacy of males in the Indian family? In society at large?

Why were a man's and a woman's *dharma* considered to be distinct?

Jain Primary Source:

The Henpecked Monk: The *Sutrakrtanga*

Why did Jainism fail to gain the wide following Hinduism and Buddhism claimed in India? What evidence do you see for that tendency here?

What similarity do you see between this passage, the earlier excerpt from the *Law of Manu*, and certain statements about women attributed to the Buddha?

Hindu Primary Source:

The Origins of the Universe: The Rigveda

Many of the world's creation stories begin with water. How does that element figure here?

What is a Veda? Why is the Rigveda particularly important for our understanding of India?

Buddhist Primary Sources:

How to Achieve Englightenment: The Sermon at Benares

Summarize the four noble truths in your own words.

Why is Buddha sometimes referred to as a reformer of Hinduism? What principles did he accept from the earlier religion? Is *karma* important here?

According to this document, had Gautama himself reached *Nirvana* at the time he delivered this sermon?

Hindu Primary Sources:

The Dilemma of Arjuna: The Bhagavadgita

In Hinduism, what did the god Vishnu represent?

What moral dilemma does Arjuna face? How is he directed to resolve it? Is this resolution acceptable from your own moral standpoint? Why or why not?

What was the original meaning of the word *yoga*?

The Monkey-King in Sri Lanka: The Ramayana

Why was the Ramayana so popular with Indian audiences? What distinguishes this epic from the contemporaneous Mahabharata?

What evidence does this document provide for attentiveness to female sexuality in Indian art and literature?

VI. Artwork

Harappan Art:

Harappan Sculpture

How does this Harappan sculpture differ from sculptures that were produced in Mesopotamia?

Harappan Seals

Why would domestic animals have figured prominently on Harappan seals?

Does the Harappan script appear to be pictographic?

What might the decipherment of this script contribute to our understanding of Harappan culture?

Naked Dancer

What evidence does this sculpture present concerning technology in Mohenjo-Daro?

Do we have any evidence that the woman portrayed would have belonged to a caste system if she actually lived in Mohenjo-Daro?

Mohenjo-Daro photograph

In what respects was Mohenjo-Daro comparable to a modern city?

How did Mohenjo-Daro get its (modern) name?

Hindu Art:

Female Earth Spirit

What commonalitites of style, form, and subject exist between Harappan sculpture and this much later female earth spirit?

Is this type of idealization of the human figure comparable to the idealization of Egyptian pharaohs? Why or why not?

What evidence does this sculpture provide for the extreme polytheism Hinduism represents?

Dancing Siva

Why was Siva originally known as "the Destroyer"? What aspects later accrued to this deity?

Is Siva male or female? Why might the artist have created a sculpture that leaves such categorization ambiguous?

Who are the other primary gods of Hinduism, and what do they represent?

Buddhist Art:

A Buddhist Prayer Hall

What elements of the Indian tradition of asceticism do you see expressed in this chamber?

How do the changes in this prayer hall over time parallel the changes in Buddhism from the time immediately after Gautama's death to its ascendancy in India under Asoka?

Asoka's Pillar

How might the Buddha have responded to such a monument commemorating his life?

What purpose, other than a religious one, did such monuments serve?

Compare this pillar to the Stele of Hammurabi from Chapter One. Is Asoka making any indirect statement about himself with such a monument?

The Lions of Sarnath

Why is the wheel under these lions' paws an apt symbol for Buddha's law? Why are the lions depicted standing firmly on top of the wheel?

When Gautama first preached in the deer park near Varanasi, what did he say?

Sanchi Gate and Stupa

How was the arc of heaven, represented in the curved shape of this stupa, represented the Buddhist prayer hall above?

How do the elaborately carved four gates recall the Lions of Sarnath above?

This monument was designed with a circular path surrounding the stupa; believers walked this in silent meditation. Why is this appropriate activity in the presence of one of his relics?

The Ideal Buddhist Couple

Identify the features of this sculptural pair that link them to both Buddhism and Hinduism.

What aspects of Indian wisdom literature find visual expression here?

VII. Identifying Important Concepts Behind the Conclusion

The Conclusion to this chapter recalls the following key ideas:

1. Indus Valley civilization

2. Aryans

3. Mauryan dynasty

4. Hinduism and Buddhism

Review these general concepts before moving on to the next chapter.

Chapter Three: China in Antiquity

I. Outlining the Chapter

Land and People of China

Dawn of Chinese Civilization: Shang Dynasty
- Political Organization
- Social Structures

The Zhou Dynasty
- Political Structures
- Economy and Society
- Hundred Schools of Ancient Philosophy
  - Confucianism
  - Legalism
  - Daoism
  - Popular Beliefs

Rise of the Chinese Empire: Qin and Han
- Qin Dynasty (221-206 B.C.E.)
  - Beyond the Frontier: Nomadic Peoples and the Great Wall of China
  - Fall of the Qin
- Glorious Han Dynasty (202 B.C.E. - 221 C.E.)
  - Confucianism and the State
  - Society and Economy in the Han Empire
  - Decline and Fall of the Han

Daily Life in Ancient China
- Humble Estate: Women in Ancient China

World of Culture
- Metalwork and Sculpture
- Language and Literature
- Music

Conclusion

II. Terms and Persons To Know

Yellow River

Yangtze River

northern frontier

Xia dynasty

Shang dynasty

Xinjiang

oracle bones

anthropomorphism

clans

Zhou dynasty

guo

Rites of Zhou

mandate of Heaven

social classes

water control projects

agricultural advances

silk

"hundred schools" of ancient philosophy

Heaven

yang and *yin*

Yi Jing

Confucius

Analects

dao

Mencius

Legalism

Daoism

Lao Tzu

Dao De Jing

popular beliefs

"Period of the Warring States"

Qin dynasty

Qin Shi Huangdi

officials

centralization

Xiongnu

Great Wall

Han dynasty

Liu Bang or Han Gaozu

civil service examination

State Confucianism

farming and trade policies

territorial expansion

Wang Mang

Xin dynasty

Cao Cao

filial piety

the "five relationships"

Bao-jia system

houses

diet

Chang'an

sexual roles

Shang bronzes

tomb of Qin Shi Huangdi

Chinese characters

calligraphy

"literary Chinese"

music

sheng

III. Mapwork

Map. 3.1. Shang China

Locate on this map the Yellow and Yangtze Rivers, sites of the two earliest river valley civilizations in China.

What was the importance of the city Anyang to the Shang dynasty?

Which of the capital cities of the later Zhou dynasty appears on this map? Was this their eastern or western capital?

Map 3.2. China during the Period of the Warring States

Why were these principalities Qu, Wu, and Yue originally formed? Which dynasty had accomplished this division?

How did the rivalries between the Qu, Wu, and Yue states lead to the formation of the Qin dynasty?

Where was the state of Qin located?

Map 3.3. The Han Empire

Why were fortifications originally built on the northern frontier of China? Why did India face a similar problem from the north?

Which of the Chines emperors is credited with building the Great Wall? Is this legend or fact? To what dynasty did he belong?

How far did Han emperors extend China's boundaries to the south, north, and west?

Map 3.4. Trade Routes of the Ancient World

Which of China's dynasties is especially known for its major expansion of trade? What restrictions did this same dynasty place on Chinese merchants?

With which countries did ancient China enjoy a beneficial trade relationship? What Chinese goods were especially prized by others?

From which foreign countries did China import wine? tortoiseshell? weapons? Which countries bought Chinese slaves and glassware?

How were goods transported along the Silk Road? What other routes were available? How far west did Chinese trade extend?

IV. Datework

Chapter Timeline: First Settled Agriculture to Han dynasty

How much later than the civilizations of Mesopotamia and Egypt does China's first organized state, the Shang dynasty, begin?

Do the Neolithic revolution and the Bronze Age also begin later in China than they did in Mesopotamia and Egypt? What about India?

Chronologically order these dynasties: Qin, Zhou, Shang, and Han. During which dynasty did Confucius live?

Approximately when does the invention of writing occur in China? The iron plow? To which two dynasties do these innovations belong?

Chronology: Ancient China

Why is the Shang dynasty considered China's first organized state?

What factors led to the collapse of the Shang dynasty? The Zhou? The Qin? The Han? Are the factors different, or are there issues that continue to confront Chinese governments throughout antiquity?

What motivated Wang Mang to seize power from the Han court?

V. Primary Sourcework

Han Primary Source:

A Treatise on the Yellow River and Its Canals: Sima Qian, *Historical Records*

Why might we expect the Yellow River to feature prominently in early accounts of Chinese accomplishments?

After the (possibly legendary) Yu, which other Chinese emperors are concerned with water control and land reclamation?

Why do these same concerns occupy ancient Mesopotamian, Egyptian, and Indian societies?

Which other (possibly legendary) emperors are credited with early technological advances?

Zhou Primary Sources:

Life in the Fields: The Book of Songs

Throughout Chinese history, the peasants or farm laborers underpin economy and society. What other classes exist? What is their relation to each other?

What evidence does this document provide for the "well field system" practiced under the Zhou dynasty?

Is there any reference to the "Big Rat" here? Why not? Who most likely authored this anonymous song? Who would have been its intended audience?

Environmental Concerns in Ancient China: The Book of Mencius

In what ways is Mencius counselling his emperor to forego short-term gain for long-term prosperity? Did the Zhou emperors heed this advice?

Why is Mencius concerned that the emperor "not interfere" with agricultural workers or their fields during the growing season? What form might such interference have taken?

What evidence do you see here for the traditional value placed on filial piety? For the "five relationships"?

Confucian Primary Source:

The Way of the Great Learning

Why is an understanding of Confucius considered vital to any study of Chinese history? What relevance do his ideas have in today's China?

Is *The Great Learning* part of the *Analects*?

What is Confucius teaching about the *dao* here? How is this Chinese concept being translated into English? How else might this word be translated?

What, according to Confucius, was the highest good?

What were the differences between Confucius' philosophy the philosophies of Legalism and Daoism?

Daoist Primary Source:

The Daoist Answer to Confucianism: *The Way of the Dao*

Putting content aside for the moment, describe the stylistic difference between Confucian and Daoist writings. How does this difference in presentation reflect these philosophies' very different goals?

What is the legendary Lao Tzu teaching about the *dao* here?

Daoist philosphers and painters valued nature very highly. What evidence do you see for that emphasis here?

How do these excerpts reflect the universal principles *yang* and *yin*?

Late Zhou Primary Source:

The Art of War: Selections from Sun Tzu

What do the ideas of Sun Tzu have in common with Legalism?

Who is the intended audience of this work?

What is Sun Tzu teaching about the *dao* here? How is his conception of the *dao* different from that of Confucius or Lao Tzu?

What quality does Sun Tzu most prize in a general, knowledge or boldness? Why?

Qin Primary Source:

Memorandum on the Burning of Books: Sima Qian, *Historical Records*

What does Li Su fear about the publication of independent opinions by conflicting philosophical schools?

Whos is excepted from the book-burning decree Li Su proposes? Why?

What books are to be spared? What books are especially censured? Why? (For the *Book of Odes*, see the Zhou primary source below.)

What punishments does the author suggest Qin Shi Huangdi inflict on those who disobey? How would not only the decree, but these punishments, have benefitted the emperor?

Zhou Primary Source:

Love Spurned in Ancient China: The *Book of Songs*: The Odes

What opportunities outside of marriage would have existed for the female singer of this song?

To what class would the married pair have belonged?

What is revealed about ancient Chinese popular religion in the second stanza?

In light of "the five relationships," in the penultimate stanza, why does the female singer indicate that she will return home, but will not tell her brothers of her husband's misbehavior?

VI. Artwork

Shang Dynasty Art:

Shell and Bone Writing

Does the writing on oracle shells and bones resemble the characters in the Chinese alphabet?

The messages on these oracles were usually in the form of a question; the crack indicated the gods' answers. What might the questions of an early emperor have been? Of a common person?

What evidence do these oracle materials provide about early Chinese belief in anthropomorphic gods?

Shang Bronzes

How were the Shang bronzes produced?

For what other purposes did Shang artisans and craftsmen use this alloy?

What does the existence of such vessels indicate about early Chinese ancestor worship? About their conception of life after death?

Qin Dynasty:

Qin Shi Huangdi

For what achievments is Qin Shi Huangdi considered one of the most influential emperors of China?

Why is he also considered one of its most ruthless emperors?

Which of the "hundred schools" of philosophy influenced him most?

The Great Wall

What did the Chinese call the nomads who lived to the north? At what periods in Chinese history did they represent the greatest threat?

Why is Qin Shi Huangdi remembered as the builder of the Great Wall? In what sense is this true?

For what other work of monumental architecture is the First Emperor of Qin most remembered?

Han Art:

Han Gentlemen

What signs of status do you perceive in the various costumes of these gentlemen? If they all belong to the same social class, what do the differences represent?

Is there any evidence to indicate whether these men are merchants, officials, or scholars?

Jade Burial Suit

During the Han dynasty, jade was believed to possess magical powers of protection, and perhaps even to impart immortality. How is this reminiscent of ancient Egyptian beliefs and funerary practices?

Agricultural photograph:

Flooded Rice Fields

How do the requirements of intensive rice farming influence the traditional Chinese family unit?

How does rice farming help to explain the value placed on cooperation and loyalty?

Han Art:

Han Pottery House

What picture of Chinese ancestor worship and the afterlife emerges when this artwork is considered together with the Shang bronzes, and Han jade suit, and the tomb and tomb soldier of Qin Shi Huangdi?

Pottery houses are found in the tombs of both sexes. Given the dual roles of men and women in Chinese society, what grave goods would you expect to find in the tombs of males? Of females?

A Bronze Horse

Compare this bronze horse to the Shang bronze vessel above. What advances have been made in bronze casting in the period between the Shang and Han dynasties?

Is this an idealized or realistic representation of a horse? Why is it balanced on a swallow? Is that an idealized or realistic portrayal of a horse's speed?

Qin Art:

Qin Shi Huangdi's Tomb

How far outside the burial mound of the First Emperor of Qin have archaeologists found terra-cotta soldiers?

What other objects were buried in the underground mausoleum complex? Why?

How was Qin Shi Huangdi's purpose similar to that of an Old Kingdom Pharaoh building his pyramid? How was it different?

Tomb Soldier (Qin Shi Huangdi's Tomb)

Do the individualized features on the terra-cotta soldiers' faces support of refute the theory that these figures are intended to replace actual human sacrifices?

At what stage of progress are the archaeological excavations of this complex today?

VII. Identifying Important Concepts Behind the Conclusion

The Conclusion to this chapter recalls the following key ideas:

1. emergence and Shang dynasty

2. Han dynasty: expansion and ideology

3. northern frontier concerns

Review these general concepts, along with the Zhou and Qin dynasties, and Legalist and Daoist philosophies, before moving on to the next chapter.

Chapter Four: The Civilization of the Greeks

I. Outlining the Chapter

Early Greece
- Minoan Crete
- Mycenaean Greeks

Greeks in a Dark Age (c. 1100 - c. 750 B.C.E.)
- Homer

World of the Greek City-States (c. 750 - c. 500 B.C.E.)
- *Polis*
- Colonization and the Rise of Tyrants
- Sparta
- Athens

High Point of Greece Civilization: Classical Greece
- Challenge of Persia
- Growth of an Athenian Empire in the Age of Pericles
- Great Peloponnesian War and the Decline of the Greek States
- Culture of Classical Greece
    - Writing of History
    - Greek Drama
    - Arts: The Classical Ideal
    - Greek Love of Wisdom
- Greek Religion
- Daily Life in Classical Athens

Rise of Macedonia and the Conquests of Alexander
- Alexander the Great
    - Legacy of Alexander

World of the Hellenistic Kingdoms
- Economic and Social Trends

Culture in the Hellenistic World
- New Directions in Literature and Art
- Golden Age of Science
- Philosophy: New Schools of Thought
- Religion in the Hellenistic World

Conclusion

II. Terms and Persons To Know

geography

topography

Minoan Crete

Arthur Evans

Knossus

Mycenean Greece

Heinrich Schliemann

Dorians

Dark Age

Ionians

iron

alphabet

Homer

Iliad

Trojan war

Odyssey

arete

polis

acropolis

agora

hoplites

colonization

tyrants

Sparta

Messenia

helots

reforms of Lycurgus

Peloponnesian League

Athens

Solon

Pisistratus

reforms of Cleisthenes

democracy

Classical Greece

Persian War

Darius

Marathon

Xerxes

Thermopylae

Salamis

Plataea

Delian League

Pericles

ostracism

Peloponnesian War

Herodotus

historia

Thucydides

tragedy

Thespis

Aeschylus

Sophocles

Euripides

Aristophanes

temples

Doric, Ionic, and Corinthian orders

Parthenon

Polyclitus

philosophy

sophists

Socrates

"Socratic method"

Plato

Forms

The Republic

Aristotle

Olympian religion

Delphi

male citizens

women

homosexuality

Philip II of Macedonia

Alexander the Great

Alexandria

Hellenistic kingdoms

Pergamum

Theocritus

Menander

Archimedes

Epicureanism

Stoicism

mystery religions

Isis

III. Mapwork

Map 4.1. Classical Greece

Which island was the center of Minoan culture? Where was the most important stronghold of Mycenaean Greece? Where is Troy? What is the importance of that city for our understanding of Mycenaean culture? Which archaeologist unearthed this city?

In what regions on this map did the Ionian Greeks live? The Aeolians? The Dorians?

What role does Messenia play in Spartan history?

What was the importance of Mt. Olympus for Greek religion? Locate this site, along with the oracle of Delphi, on this map. Where were the Olympic festivals founded? For what purpose?

Where did the Greeks live in relation to the Persians? Note the location of Marathon, Thermopylae, Plataea and Salamis. What importance did these sites play in the Persian War?

Regarding the Peloponnesian War, locate Athens and Sparta. Which city-state dominated the Peloponnesian League? The Delian League? What happened at Aegospotami?

Map 4.2. The Conquests of Alexander the Great

Where on this map was Alexander born? What regions had his father, Philip II, already subdued? Why, when he succeeded to the throne of Macedonia, did Alexander's ambitions lead him east rather than west?

What city did Alexander designate as the administrative capital of his empire?

Why was Alexander unsuccessful in conquering India?

Looking back at the maps from the first three chapters, do you see any empires as large as Alexander's? Why was Alexander so successful? How did Homer serve as inspiration to him?

Where did Alexander die?

Map 4.3. The World of the Hellenistic Monarchs

After Alexander's death, how was his empire divided? Was any territory lost between the time of his death and the formation of the succeeding Hellenistic monarchies? (Refer back to Map 4.2.)

Why is this world called "Hellenistic" rather than "Greek" or "Macedonian" after Alexander? What united these kingdoms?

IV. Datework

Chapter timeline: Mycenaean Greece to the Hellenistic Kingdoms

When did the civilization of Minoan Crete flourish? Were the Mycenaeans solely responsible for their downfall? Why is the period immediately following the Mycenaeans referred to as a Dark Age?

Which period in Greek history do the Persian Wars initiate? Which of these eras begins with the empire of Alexander the Great?

It is clear from this timeline that the philosophers Plato and Aristotle belonged to the Classical Age of Greece. When did the philosophers Epicurus and Zeno live, and with which philosophical schools are they associated?

After the Lycurgan reforms, when did the reforms of Solon and Cleisthenes occur? Are the three movements related?

Chronology: The Persian Wars

Against which Persian king did the Ionians unsuccessfully revolt in 499?

Why did the Athenians consider the battle of Marathon so important to their own history?

The Spartans and Athenians cooperated against the Persians. Which of the major battles was won primarily by Spartan land forces? By Athenian navy?

Which of the Classical Greek historians chronicled this war?

Chronology: The Great Peloponnesian War

When the war began in 431, both Athens and Sparta were confident of victory. On what factors did each side base their optimism?

Why did Athens and Sparta come into conflict?

What power to the north later took advantage of the Greek states' weakness after this costly war?

Which of the Classical Greek historians chronicled this war?

Chronology: The Rise of Macedonia and the Conquests of Alexander

What did Alexander accomplish at the Battles of Issus and Gaugamela?

How old was Alexander when he died?

V. Primary Sourcework

Eighth-Century primary source:

Homer's Ideal of Excellence: Homer, *Iliad*

What does Hector hope for his son? How do his hopes reflect his status as warrior-aristocrat rather than hoplite soldier? With which two periods of Greek history are these two types of strategy associated?

Do the *Iliad* and *Odyssey* describe solely the Mycenaean age? According to the discoveries of Heinrich Schliemann, when did the Trojan war take place?

What values did later Greeks find in Homer? What about Hector makes him an example of *arete*? How does Andromache exemplify *arete* for women?

Spartan primary source:

The Lycurgan Reforms: Plutarch, *Lycurgus*

What was a Spartan mother's role in bringing up her sons? Were fathers' roles different? According to legend, for what purpose did a woman bear sons?

Why were the boys raised in a group? How old were they when their serious training began? How much intellectual training did they receive?

Why were Spartan boys encouraged to steal their food? What skills would such activity develop?

Why would this whole program have been distasteful to the Athenians?

Would Athenians have agreed with Spartan women's activities?

Classical primary sources:

Athenian Democracy: The Funeral Oration of Pericles from Thucydides, *History of the Peloponnesian War*

How does Pericles define democracy? What two ancient Greek words form this English term?

Is it possible that Thucydides was present at this actual speech? What reporting techniques did Thucydides use in his search for accuracy in his history?

Why would the Athenian passion for debate described by Pericles have been distasteful to the Spartans? On the other hand, how does eagerness for discussion perfectly suit democracy?

According to this document, why did the Athenians feel justified to dominate the Delian League and to use it for purposes of Athenian imperialism?

What is the meaning of the Greek word *historia*? How did Herodotus and Thucydides see this activity differently?

Athenian Comedy: Sex as an Antiwar Instrument from Aristophanes, *Lysistrata*

How is Lysistrata's name especially appropriate? Why is Kalonike, whose name means "beautiful victory," having trouble taking this oath?

What other types of play were presented at the yearly festivals for Dionysus in Athens? How did the genres differ?

What political message did Aristophanes present in *Lysistrata*? Who did he satirize in *The Clouds*?

Household Management and the Role of the Athenian Wife: Xenophon, *Oeconomicus*

It would not have been unusual for an Athenian husband to be twice the age of his wife. How do you see age difference reflected in this document?

What evidence does this document provide for romantic love between married couples? Why do you suppose that is so?

Do you agree with Xenophon's view that women were "less capable of...endurance" than men? Did men have a smaller portion of "affection for new-born babes"? What about today?

Hellenistic primary sources:

The Destruction of the Persian Palace at Persepolis: Arrian, *The Life of Alexander the Great* and Diodorus of Siciliy, *Library of History*

Which of these accounts do you find more plausible? Why?

Which author lived closer to the time of Alexander himself? Does this influence your answer to the above question? Why or why not?

A New Autonomy for Women: Letter from Isias to Hephaistion, 168 B.C.E., and Letter from Ktesikles to King Ptolemy, 220 B.C.E.

How has Hephaistion's child been supported in his father's absence?

Why does Ktesikles accuse his daughter of wrongdoing? For what does he blame Dionysios? What does he ask of Ptolemy and Diophanes?

What arguments might Nike have made on her own behalf?

The Stoic Ideal of Harmony with God: Cleanthes, *Hymn to Zeus*

What features of this hymn identify it as Stoic?

According to Cleanthes, what defines a "bad mortal"? By implication, what would define a good one?

How did Stoicism differ from the Hellenistic philosophy Epicureanism?

VI. Artwork

Minoan Art:

The Minoan Sport of Bull Leaping

Archaeological excavation has indicated that the Palace of Knossus was abandoned in great haste, and few bodies were found in the ruins. Does this more strongly support either the tsunami theory or the Mycenaean theory about its destruction?

When the Minoans and the Mycenaeans came into conflict, what military advantages did each side possess? What types of archaeological evidence give us this picture of each side?

Do you see evidence in this artwork for a strong cultural tie with Egypt? Geographically speaking, what is the connection between Crete and Egypt?

Mycenaean Art:

The So-Called Death Mask of Agamemnon

Why has this work of art been designated only the "so-called" Death Mask of Agamemnon? What Homer's *Iliad* makes historical claims about Agamemnon and the other Greek heroes difficult?

Schliemann's records indicate that he also found a treasure hoard of women's golden jewelry. He called this find "The Treasure of Helen." Why did he give the objects this name?

What did Schliemann believe about Troy?

Seventh-Century Art:

The Hoplite Forces

What is the advantage of hoplite battle over individual aristocratic duels? What are some disadvantages?

What were the social consequences of the adoption of hoplite warfare? Does this relate to the rise of democracy within the city-states?

Classical Art:

Pericles: Roman Copy of Fifth-Century Bronze Original

Why is understanding the role of Pericles in fifth-century Athens crucial for our understanding of the outbreak of the Peloponnesian War?

Why has the sculptor chosen to depict Pericles with his helmet on, but raised to reveal his face?

How did the political and military career of Pericles exemplify *arete* within the *polis*?

Doric, Ionic, and Corinthian Orders

What order of column adorns the Parthenon?

According to legend, one of the orders developed from a stylization of ram's horns, another from acanthus leaves, and another from a stripped tree trunk. Which developed from which natural feature?

The Parthenon

Why is the Parthenon frequently cited as a prime example of the classical ideal in architecture?

Where did the funds originate for the building of this temple?

The Parthenon stands on the acropolis of the city of Athens; beneath it lies the *agora*. Review the meaning of these two terms within the classical *polis*.

Doryphoros

Why is the *Doryphoros* frequently cited as a prime example of the classical ideal in sculpture?

Compare this example with the previous bust of Pericles. How do both scrulptures artistically represent the concept of *arete*?

How did classical sculpture differ from Hellenistic sculpture?

Women in the Loom Room

What did citizenship for women consist of if they had no rights and were barred from any political activity?

How does the scene on the vase reflect women's roles in Athens? How were women's roles in Sparta different?

Compare this scene with the primary source excerpt of Xenophon's *Oeconomicus*. How does this artwork support the text?

Hellenistic Art:

Bust of Alexander the Great

Many ancient Greek sculptures, such as this bust of Alexander and the bust of Pericles above, survive only in Roman copies (the original is no longer extant). Why did the Romans make so many copies of Greek originals?

Is this what Alexander really looked like? What elements of classical idealism do you see here? Hellenistic realism?

How would Alexander's identification with the heroes Achilles and Heracles have promoted his political and military ambitions?

Portrait of Queen Arsinoe¨ II

How does this statue represent a combination of Greek and Egyptian elements?

Why is such a combination well suited to commemorate the role Arsinoë II played in the Hellenistic world?

How does the career of Arsinoë II reflect the new roles of Hellenistic women?

Old Market Woman

As Hellenistic sculptors moved away from the classical ideal toward more emotional concerns, Hellenistic religion and philosophy were also undergoing significant changes. How do the concerns of the mystery religions, Epicureanism and Stoicism parellel the transformation of Classical to Hellenistic art?

Compare this statue with the *Doryphoros* above, and point out specific differences in style.

Why is the *Doryphoros* nude, while the Old Market Woman is clothed?

The Cult of Isis

What political events make it possible for an Egyptian religion to become a popular cult all around the Mediterranean world?

Why was the Isis cult attractive to believers? Why would it have been especially appealing to the lower classes? To slaves? To women?

How did the mystery religions differ from Olympian religion?

VII. Identifying Important Concepts Behind the Conclusion

The Conclusion to this chapter recalls the following key ideas:

1. Ancient Greece as the fountainhead of Western culture: philosophy, literature, art, science, democracy

2. Political struggles

3. Hellenistic world

Review these general concepts before moving on to the next chapter.

Chapter Five: The Roman World

I. Outlining the Chapter

Emergence of Rome
- Greeks and Etruscans
- Early Rome

Roman Republic
- Roman Conquest of Italy
- Roman State
    - Struggle of the Orders: Social Divisions in the Roman Republic

Roman Conquest of the Mediterranean (264-133 B.C.E.)
- Punic Wars
- Eastern Mediterranean
- Nature of Roman Imperialism

Decline and Fall of the Roman Republic (133-31 B.C.E.)
- New Role for the Roman Army: Marius and Sulla
- Collapse of the Republic

Age of Augustus (31 B.C.E. -- 14 C.E.)
- Augustan Society

Early Empire (14-180)
- The Five "Good Emperors" (96-180)
- Roman Empire at Its Height: Frontiers and the Provinces
- Prosperity in the Early Empire

Culture and Society in the Roman World
- Roman Literature
- Art
- Roman Law
- Roman Family
- Slaves and Their Masters
- Imperial Rome
- Gladitorial Shows

Religion in the Roman World: The Rise of Christianity
- Jewish Background
- Rise of Christianity

Decline and Fall of the Roman Empire
- Reforms of Diocletian and Constantine
- Triumph of Christianity
- Fall of the Western Roman Empire

Conclusion

II. Terms and Persons To Know

geography

Greeks

Etruscans

Romulus and Remus

Latin

seven kings

Sacred Way

Republic

Livy

Gauls

Roman confederation

conquest of Italy

consuls

praetors

imperium

senate

assemblies

struggle of the orders

patricians

plebeians

plebescita

Carthage

Punic Wars

Hannibal

Africa

Macedonia

imperialism

nobiles

optimates

populares

latifundia

Tiberius and Gaius Gracchus

Marius

Sulla

First Triumvirate

Julius Caesar

Octavian

Antony

Cleopatra VII

Battle of Actium

princeps

imperator

legates

three classes: senatorial, equestrian, lower

social legislation

Julio-Claudian dynasty

"five good emperors"

frontiers

provinces

trade, industry and agriculture

Greek culture

Plautus

Catullus

Cicero

"golden age" of literature

Virgil

Horace

Ovid

Livy's *History of Rome*

"silver age" of literature

Seneca

Tacitus

sculpture

architecture and roads

Roman Law

Twelve Tables

praetors

jurists

paterfamilias

slavery

city of Rome

insulae

gladitorial shows

ampitheatres

state religion

mystery religions

Mithras

Judaea

Jesus of Nazareth

Christos

Paul of Tarsus

gospels

New Testament

Diocletian

Constantine

illustres and *illustrissimi*

rise of Christianity

Edict of Milan

Theodosius "the Great"

Germanic tribes

"decline and fall of the Roman Empire:" possible causes

III. Mapwork

Map 5.1. Ancient Italy and the City of Rome

What was the importance of the Etruscans (centered in Etruria) to the early history of Rome? The Sabines? The Samnites?

Where did the Gauls come from? What danger did they pose to early Rome?

Why was the southern portion of the Italian peninsula called Magna Graecia, after Greek culture?

According to the legend Livy records, where did Horatius make his stand?

Map 5.2. Roman Conquests in the Mediterranean

By the close of the Punic Wars and the wars in the Eastern Mediterranean, how much of the Mediterranean world fell under Roman control? How much of this land originally had belonged to the empire of Alexander?

By what means did the Romans gain Spain in the west? The Carthaginian territory in north Africa? Greece? Pergamum?

Why did the Romans destroy Corinth in 146 B.C.?

Map 5.3. The Roman Empire from 14 to 117

How much territory accrued to the Roman Empire during the first two centuries C.E.? (Refer back to Map 5.2.)

Was this due to a purposeful imperialistic program, or to other causes?

Why did Augustus say that the empire was big enough, and should grow no larger? Why did Trajan disagree, and pursue further expansion?

How did Egypt come into Roman hands?

Did the Romans ever hold Ireland? Scotland? For what purpose was Hadrian's wall built?

What made Byzantium such an important city for trade?

Map 5.4. Imperial Rome

According to legend, who founded the city of Rome (and constructed the original city walls)?

Which of the Ways (roads) shown here was the first road built in Rome?

Why was Rome beautified by the emperors with so many public buildings, including ampitheatres, racetracks, and baths?

What purposes did acqueducts serve? *Insulae*? How many people are estimated to have lived in Rome at its height? What urban problems arose as a result?

Who were the praetorians (note their facilities in the northeast area of Rome).

In the history of ancient Rome, what groups successfully breached its defensive walls?

Map 5.5. Divisions of the Restored Roman Empire

What were the reforms of Diocletian? What problems did he intend to solve?

What language was commonly spoken in the western regions of the empire? In the east? What were the primary administrative cities in each region?

Who was placed in charge of the new prefectures? By what means did they govern?

Why did Constantine change the name of the city Byzantium? Why did he not live in Rome, as past emperors had done?

IV. Datework

Chapter Timeline: From the Roman Republic to the Fall of Rome

What year is considered to mark the end of the Roman Republic and the beginning of the Roman Empire or Imperial period? Why?

What causes bring about the fall of Rome in the fifth century C.E.?

What part did Jesus of Nazareth play in the Roman legacy to western civilization? In what Roman province was he born?

How does the struggle of the orders influence the structure of Roman government?

Chronology: The Roman Conquest of Italy and the Mediterranean

How did the creation of the Roman confederation lead to Roman possession of the entire Italian peninsula?

What was the importance of the Battle of Cannae during the Punic Wars? Why did this not secure victory for Hannibal? What happened at the Battle of Zama?

Why did Cato, down to the year 146 B.C.E., end his speeches to the senate with the phrase, "Carthage must be destroyed"?

Rome had declared Greece free in 196 B.C.E. Why then is Macedonia declared a Roman province in 148 B.C.E.?

Which of these events listed here represent conquests in Italy? In Africa? In the east? What progression do you see developing?

Chronology: The Decline and Fall of the Republic

What efforts did the Gracchus brothers make at reform? Why did the senate resist them?

What important lesson did the members of the first triumvirate learn from the success of Marius and Sulla?

What occupied Octavian between the years 44 and 31 B.C.E.? With what result?

Given the history contained on just this brief chronological outline, why would Augustus' promise of peace and stability sound very attractive to future Roman ears?

Chronology: The Late Empire -- Chief Rulers and Events

Why was the military monarchy of the Severan dynasty followed by military anarchy? What characterized the years of anarchy for the emperors of Rome?

What was the significance of the Edict of Milan? How did Theodosius carry forward what Constantine had begun with this edict?

Who was Romulus Augustulus? "Augustulus" means "little Augustus" in Latin. Given his position in the empire, why is this ironic?

Why did the Visigoths and the Vandals move southward into the Italian peninsula in the fifth century C.E.?

V. Primary Sourcework

Republican Primary Sources:

Cincinnatus Saves Rome: A Roman Morality Tale from Livy, *The Early History of Rome*

What similarities have Americans often seen between the early Roman senator Cincinnatus and the early Roman general and statesman George Washington?

What moral lesson are we to learn from Cincinnatus having resigned early from his appointment as dictator?

What Roman values are exemplified here? How are they similar to the values portrayed in the story of Horatius from Livy that introduced this chapter?

Why did Livy say he wrote his history? As a writer in the Augustan age, would he have pleased or displeased Augustus with such a purpose?

The Destruction of Carthage: Appian, *Roman History*

What "technical breach" of their treaty with Rome did the Carthaginians make that led to the Third Punic War?

Appian wrote this account of the fall of Carthage centuries after it occurred. Does this document strike you as factual? What features seem more rhetorical than realistic? How is this reminiscent of Silver Age Latin literature?

What connection does the well-educated Roman general Scipio make between Carthage, Troy, and Rome? Why?

The Assassination of Julius Caesar: Plutarch, *Life of Caesar*

What role did soothsayers have in Roman society? Why would a Roman leader consult them? What moral lesson are we to infer from the fact that this anonymous diviner was right?

Caesar had always believed Brutus to be one of his closest friends and allies. What evidence do you see for that relationship in Plutarch's account of Caesar's death?

What had been the former relationship between Caesar and Pompey? Why does this makes the scene of Caesar's death ironic?

Today, when someone takes irrevocable and momentous action, they are sometimes said to have "crossed the Rubicon." Where did this saying come from? How does it relate to Caesar's success -- and ultimate assassination?

Imperial Primary Sources:

The Fate of Cremona in the Year of the Four Emperors from Tacitus, *The Histories*

Why would a Roman general allow his troops to visit such destruction on a Roman city?

How is this scene reminiscent of the fall of Carthage as described by Arrian above? Does this account strike you as more realistic? Why? How close did Tacitus live to the events he is describing here?

What (other than the possible reasons Tacitus mentions) might have saved the temple of Mefitis when no other structure was respected?

Ovid and the Art of Love

Why did Ovid's *Art of Love* (and his *Amores*) fail to please Augustus? Was Ovid seriously recommending the conduct he described in these works? Why might this not have mattered to Augustus?

What reforms did Augustus attempt with his program of moral and social legislation? Was he successful?

Is the "woman of...choice" described in this poem married or not? What are the consequences of your answer in regard to Ovid's poetic intentions?

Was adultery a serious offence in Augustan Rome for men? For women? Why was there a distinction?

Cato the Elder on Women: Livy, *The History of Rome*

How did Roman women respond to the Oppian Law?

What particular actions on the part of the women protesting this law have angered Cato?

What more general concerns does he have about Roman women? What does he believe is women's ultimate goal in regard to men?

Some senators claimed that the Oppian Law was intended to reduce envy between the classes (since the lower class could not afford the lavish public displays enjoyed by the upper class). Women, however, felt that the law was unfairly designed to restrict their rights (since one of the few rights granted to them in Roman public life was enjoyment of their wealth). Who was right?

The Roman Fear of Slaves: Tacitus, *The Annals of Imperial Rome*

Compare this reading to the speech of Cato from Livy's history above. Whom did Roman male citizens fear more, slaves or women? Why?

What was the advice of Cato the Elder concerning the maintenance of slaves?

What was the largest slave revolt in Roman history? How did it end?

What were the worst occupations a slave could hold in Roman society? The best?

What was the approximate ratio of free persons to slaves during the time of the Empire? How were so many slaves acquired?

Explain the practice of manumission.

The Public Baths of the Roman Empire: Lucian, *Hippias, or The Bath*

Who was responsible for building the public baths of Rome? Who used them?

Note the progression from rooms of cold to warm to hot water. How is this reminiscent of a modern spa or gym?

Why were the baths designed to be not merely functional, but aesthetically appealing? What lessons might modern societies learn from such a policy?

Christian Ideals: The Sermon on the Mount

What was the Christian ideal to be, according to this gospel sermon?

Compare this sermon to the Buddha's sermon on the Four Noble Truths from Chapter Two. How are the two different? What similarities do you see?

What is the meaning of the word "gospel"? By what process did the New Testament come into existence? Why were its sources written down?

How does Jesus of Nazareth's message contrast with the Greco-Roman emphasis on ritual within polytheisic state religion? How does it compare with the message of the mystery religions?

VI. Artwork

Etruscan Art:

Etruscan Married Couple

How did the Etruscans transform the city of Rome? What geographical and political factors made such influence possible?

Roman Art:

A Roman Legionary

What length of military service did the Roman government demand of its male citizens? How did this change over time?

What relation did legionary battle tactics have to those of the Greek phalanx?

What role did the Roman legions play in the success of Marius? Of Sulla? Of Julius Caesar? In the death of Nero? In the successes of Trajan and Titus?

Why did the army become so important a method of movement from the lower class upward? How did generals reward their troops for service?

Caesar

What evidence do you see here that Roman portraiture was known for not only its realism, but for its attention to realistic (even if unattractive) detail?

Who else belonged to the first triumvirate? What happened to dissolve this group?

Why was Caesar assassinated? What did his killers believe they could accomplish by his death?

Augustus

When did Octavian receive the title Augustus? What does it mean in Latin? Why did the senate grant it to him?

The Julio-Claudians claimed descent from the Roman goddess Venus, the goddess of love. What reminder has the sculptor added to this portrait to impress viewers of this fact?

Does Augustus' dress bear any resemblance to the dress of the Roman legionary above? After noting similarities, account for the differences you see.

Is this a realistic statue? An idealizing one? How might this statue be complimentary to Augustus' preferred role, that of *princeps*?

The Shipping of Grain

Even though it is not marked, find the location of Ostia on Map 5.1.

How did the ship depicted here get the first part of its name? What might this imply about the man whose tomb included this painting?

What products were important in Roman export? Import?

Why was the importation of grain so crucial to the urban population of Rome from the timeof Augustus onward?

Roman Theatre: Rehearsal of a Greek Play

Why are these actors in a Roman painting rehearsing a Greek play rather than a Roman one?

Why were Greek New Comedy plots so popular with audiences?

In what other art forms were Greek precedents influential?

Interior of the Colosseum of Rome

This photograph shows the hollow tunnels that ran underneath the original floor of the arena (the floor with its trapdoors has weathered away). Why would this system have been useful in gladitorial shows?

What does the Colosseum, and other amphitheatres of this type, reveal about Roman taste in entertainment? How does this compare to modern tastes for violence in entertainment?

What was the significance of Juvenal's famous phrase about the urban poor's "bread and circuses"? Does this have any relevance in cities today?

A Roman Lady

Why did Roman males believe that women required guardianship?

How did Roman women achieve a measure of power, influence, and freedom in spite of this persistent belief?

This villa has been uncovered by archaeological excavations in the region of Pompeii, a city buried by volcanic eruption in 79 C.E. Why is this eruption so important for our understanding of the Roman empire today?

The Gladitorial Games

Ancient sources indicate that in Pompeii, the ampitheatre was closed because of a public riot that followed certain games. Why might such entertainments as are pictured here result in disorder?

What species do you see represented here? What impact did the games have on wildlife within the Roman empire?

Christ and His Apostles

The catacombs were underground tunnels used by the early Christians for burial. What societal pressures led them to create catacombs? Was such pressure constant, or sporadic? Why?

Explain the role the following figures played in regard to the early Christian church: Peter, Paul of Tarsus, Nero, Constantine.

VII. Identifying Important Concepts Behind the Conclusion

The Conclusion to this chapter recalls the following key ideas:

1. Rise of the Roman Empire up to the domination of Octavian (Augustus)

2. Roman achievements: language, law, engineering, government

3. Christianity and the Germanic invasions

Review these general concepts, and study the Reflection which follows this chapter, before moving on to the next chapter.

Chapter Six: The New World

I. Outlining the Chapter

First Americans

Early Civilizations in Central America
- Teotihuacán: America's First Metropolis
- Mysterious Maya
  - Mayan Hieroglyphs
  - Mystery of Mayan Decline
- Aztecs
  - Politics and Society
  - Land of the Feathered Serpent: Aztec Religion and Culture
  - Destruction of Aztec Civilization

First Civilizations in South America
- Inca
  - World of the Four Quarters: Inca Politics and Society
  - Inca Culture

Stateless Societies in the New World

Conclusion

II. Terms and Persons To Know

Bering Strait

Amerindians

Mesoamerica

Olmec culture

Monte Alban

Teotihuacán

Pyramid of the Sun

pulque

obsidian

chinampas

Yucatán peninsula

Maya

Diego de Landa

John Lloyd Stephens and Frederick Catherwood

cacao tree

Tikal and Copan

"big men"

Itzamna

human sacrifice

ball court

class system

Mayan hieroglyphic writing

"Long Count"

Palenque

Temple of Inscriptions

Pacal

decline of Mayan culture

Toltecs

Kukulcan

Quetzalcoatl

Chichen Itza

Mexica

Aztecs

Tenochtitlán

Lake Texcoco

Huitzilopochtli

Aztec government

Bernal Díaz

class system

calpulli

sex roles

Aztec pantheon

cosmology

religious ritual

Father Diego Duran

influence of Olmec art and architecture

La Venta

Tlaloc

Stone of the Sun

glyphs

Hernán Cortés

Moctezuma Xocoyotzin

Tlaxcallan

South American geography

early Andes civilization

Chavin site

Moche

"Nazca lines"

El Niño

Chanchan

Chimor

Incas

Pachakuti

Cuzco

"world of the four quarters"

"Inca mode of production"

road system

women's roles

agriculture

Quecha

quipu

Francisco Pizarro

stateless societies in North America

Archaic period

Mississippian (Mississippi River Valley) cultures

chieftans

Cahokia

League of Iroquois

Anasazi peoples

Chaco Canyon

Pueblo Bonito

Mesa Verde

Zuni and Hopi peoples

Apache and Navajo

Arawak

Orinoco River

III. Mapwork

Map 6.1a. Peoples and Cultures of North America, and
Map 6.1b. Peoples and Cultures of Central and Latin America

What were the differences between the governmental bureaucracies and class structures of those societies termed "chiefdoms" and those which were "organized states"? How does this relate to the idea of "big men"? Of "stateless" societies?

Were the patterns of hunter-gatherer societies in the New World similar to those described at the opening of Chapter One? Why?

What crops were important to the farming peoples of North America? When did these foods begin to be produced in large-scale agricultural systems?

Was the Amazon River valley an important early center of civilization in South America? How does the development of civilization in this area compare to the earliest river valley civilizations described in Chapters One, Two, and Three? What about the developments along the Mississippi River valley?

For which Mesoamerican culture did the city of Teotihuacán serve as capital? Locate the Yucatán peninsula on this map insert.

Map. 6. 2. The Heartland of Mesoamerica

Who were the Mexica?

Why has the Yucatán peninsula been described as a "great green thumb"? What crops did the Olmecs cultivate here? Under the *Maya*, what was a *chinampa*?

Explain the significance of the following sites for Mayan history: Tikal and Copan. Who was "18 rabbit"? How many people are estimated to have lived at Tikal at its height?

Did the European arrival in the 16th century C.E. affect the Maya?

Map 6.3. The Vally of Mexico Under Aztec Rule

When Bernal Díaz climbed to the top of the pyramid of Huitzilopochtli and Tlaloc in Tenochtitlán, what did he see? What features of his description are indicated here?

What was Díaz doing in the Aztec capital city? What did the two gods whose temple he climed in order to survey the land represent?

How did the Aztec govern those peoples they conquered? Why is this information available to us today (how did it survive)? How did their tactics lead to their own downfall when Cortés arrived?

Given the position of Tenochtitlán, why was Cortés very fortunate that Moctezuma willingly allowed him to approach his palace? Why did Moctezuma do this?

Map 6.4. The Inca Empire about 1500 C.E.

What geographical and climatological features of the west coast of South America made Incan agriculture challenging? How did the farmers meet these challenges?

By what means did the Incas build their elaborate system of highways and roads? What other civic projects were undertaken according to the same method?

What had the peoples of Moche and Chimor achieved before the arrival of the Incas?

What factors are responsible for the decline of the Incas?

IV. Datework

Chapter Timeline: From the Teotihuacán kingdom to Pizarro's conquest of the Inca

Why did the organized state societies depicted here reach their flowering later than the first organized states of Mesopotamia, Egypt, India, and China?

In what ways did the cultural patterns of the Olmecs serve as a model for all later Mesoamerican civilizations?

Chronology: Early America

Where do scholars believe the first human beings in America originated? What climatological situation made this possible? Why did they venture into the New World?

When agriculture begins in the Americas, what crops are produced? How are these different from those produced at the dawn of agriculture in Mesopotamia? India? China?

What are some of the prevalent theories about the decline of Mayan civilization? How did the Aztecs come to power? The Incas?

Why did Cortés and Pizarro come to the New World? Why did they have both soldiers and priests in their retinue? Why are the priests' writings such a valuable source for scholars today?

V. Primary Sourcework

Mayan Primary Sources:

The Creation of the World: A Mayan View from the *Popol Vuh*, The Sacred Book of the Maya

When we read this excerpt from the *Popol Vuh* today, are we reading a translation of the original Mayan script? What has intervened? What consequences might this have for our understanding of the original?

What did Bishop Diego de Landa say happened to most original Mayan books?
Compare this creation narrative to that from the Book of Genesis, and to the excerpt on the origins of the universe from the Rigveda in Chapter Two. What similarities do you perceive? What important differences?

Feathers were significant in Mesoamerican societies' costumes and adornment; the "feathered serpent" features in the mythologies of this region. Why are feathers important here?

Is this a monotheistic or polytheistic document? Who creates humans? Why?

A Sample of Mayan Writing

According to the sampling of hieroglyphs shown here, what were primary concerns in Mayan culture? For what statum of society would the signs for "birth of" and "accession of" be particularly important? What about "captor of" and "he captured"?

How might the signs for captives and bloodletting be related?

What would the absence of adjectives and adverbs mean for this language? What could not be expressed as a result? Does this mean that the Mayan spoken language was similarly limited? Why would the hieroglyphic system be if the spoken language was not?

Primary Sources Concerning the Aztecs:

Markets and Merchandise in Aztec Mexico: Bernal Díaz, *The Conquest of New Spain*

Why was Díaz concerned carefully to record the wealth the Spaniards were finding in "New Spain"? Who was his intended audience?

How were the Aztecs able to command such a variety of goods for availability in their markets? What practical goods are present? Which are luxury items for the consumption of the upper class?

What surprising recycling project does Díaz record? What reaction does he expect from Spaniards who learn of this?

Aztec Religion through Spanish Eyes: Diego Duran, *History of the Indies of New Spain*

Why were Spanish observers revolted by Aztec rituals?

How do such rituals relate to the Aztec belief in a previous four worlds and their four suns? When did the Aztecs believe they were living? Was there any way to prevent the end of this world?

Who was used for human sacrifice?

A Description of Tenochtitlán: Bernal Díaz, *The Conquest of New Spain*

For what purposes were pyramids used in Aztec culture? How does this differ from their function in Egyptian society?

Locate the causeways and water supply systems Díaz described on Map 6.3.

As Díaz records, some of Cortés' troops had travelled to the great cities of the Old World, including Constantinople and Rome. What would have looked familiar to them in Tenochtitlán? What particular details may have invited Díaz to compare this city with those two particular cities of the former Roman empire?

Moctezuma's Greeting to Hernán Cortés: Hernán Cortés, Letter from Mexico

Why did Moctezuma identify Cortés with Quetzalcoatl?

Why does gold feature so prominently in these two men's first conversation?

What has Moctezuma been told in advance about information given to Cortés? Does this information seem to have disturbed him?

Inca Primary Sources:

Pachakuti, Reformer of the World: Garcilaso de la Vega, *Royal Commentaries of the Incas*

Who was Garcilaso de la Vega's intended audience? Why does this lead him to term certain games "of no great interest" and to refer to certain laws as concerning "worship of idols" and "illicit" marriages?

Does "El Inca" admire the former king Pachakuti? Why? How does he convey this in his writing?

What provisions did Pachakuti make for the very old and young? What might modern societies learn from this today?

An Incan *Aide-Mémoire*: Garcilaso de la Vega, *Royal Commentaries of the Incas*

Together, how did *quipu*, the *quipucamayus*, the *amautas*, and the *haravicus* record Incan history?

What are the strengths and fragilities of these various systems?

VI. Artwork

Teotihuacán Art:

The Pyramid of the Sun, Teotihuacán

How are the astrological concerns and astronomical skills of the Teotihuacán culture reflected in the Pyramid of the Sun?

Why was this structure built? What have archaeologists discovered beneath it?

Mayan Art:

Preparing for Sacrifice

What was the Spanish response to artifacts such as these?

What memory remained of Mayan civilization before the nineteenth-century expedition of Stephens and Catherwood? What did they find?

How do artworks such as this provide evidence for cultural links between the Teotihuacán culture, the Maya, and the Aztecs?

A Ball Court

What was the purpose of the ball courts? Where are they found?

Where would the game have been played, and where would the observers have been seated? Approximately how many people do you think this structure could have accomodated?

Why are "skull racks" sometimes found alongside these structures in Mesoamerica?

The Palace at Palenque

How does this structure compare to those found on other Mayan sites? To the structures of Teotihuacán? To Aztec sites?

What does this building indicate about the political and social structures of Mayan society?

Aztec Art:

Quetzalcoatl

Why was Quetzalcoatl an important figure in many Mesoamerican cultures?

What similarities of style do you see between this sculpture, which adorned a temple, and the Mayan hieroglyphs above? Why would such a similarity exist?

The Stone of the Fifth Sun

What religious rituals did belief in the fifth sun engender among the Aztecs?

How are these rituals reflected on the disk?

Surrounding the image of the Sun in the center is an inscription in Aztec "long count." What was this system and what was its purpose?

South American Art:

A Gold Diadem

How did the Spanish use of objects such as this diadem reflect their interest in coming to the New World?

How does this artifact document class stratification in South American societies?

Incan Art:

The Stones of Cuzco

Did the Incas (and other early societies of the New World) have the wheel? The horse? How did they transport the stones necessary for such monumental works?

What work force built these walls? What purposes did the terraces, the source of some of these stones, serve?

How long, considering how long it took to work just a few stones, would it have taken to construct this wall? What factors influence your answer?

How did the Incas first establish themselves in the Andes? Why were these walls important thereafter?

Machu Picchu

How is this site similar to other Inca sites?

What religious concerns do you see reflected here?

How did the urban population who dwelled here sustain themselves?

North American Art:

Cliff Palace at Mesa Verde

Who were the Anasazi? Who gave them this name?

Which Amerindian cultures succeeded them in the Southwest?

What food sources and agricultural products were important to the Anasazi?

Why were sites such as Mesa Verde abandoned?

VII. Identifying Important Concepts Behind the Conclusion

The Conclusion to this chapter recalls the following key ideas:

1. Human arrival in the New World: patterns of culture in Central, South, and North America
2. Comparison of New and Old World civilizations
3. European arrival

Review these general concepts, and the introduction to Part II, "New Patterns of Civilization," before moving on to the next chapter.

Chapter Seven: The World of Islam

I. Outlining the Chapter

Rise of Islam

Teachings of Muhammad

Arab Empire and Its Successors
- Umayyads
- Abbasids
- Seljuk Turks
- Crusades
- Mongols

Islamic Civilization
- Political Structures
- Wealth of Araby: Trade and Manufacturing in the Middle East
- Islamic Society
- Culture of Islam
  - Philosophy and Science
  - Islamic Literature
  - Islamic Art and Architecture

Conclusion

II. Terms and Persons To Know

Arabia

Nabataea

Bedouins

sheikh

majlis

caravan trade

Allah

Ka'aba

Muhammad

Mecca

Gabriel

Koran or Qur'an

Islam

Muslims

Khadija

Medina

Hegira

umma

monotheistic

suras

"five pillars"

ulama

Shari'ah

Hadith

Abu Bakr

caliph

jihad

Arab expansion

Muhammad Ali

Mu'awiyah

Umayyads

North Africa

Iberian Peninsula

Battle of Tours (or Poitiers)

Byzantine Empire

Damascus

Mesopotamia and Persia

Hussein

Shi'ites

Sunnites

Abu al-Abbas

Abbasid dynasty

Baghdad

Harun al-Rashid

Amin and Ma'mun

disintegration

Fatimids

Seljuk Turks

crusades

Alexius I

Saladin

Mongols

Genghis KhanHulegu

Khubilai Khan

Mamluks

Ottoman Turks

Sultan Mehmet II

Constantinople

imam

diwan

vizier

caliphate

trade

egalitarianism

slaves

women

urban life

Arabic language

philosophy

Ibn Rushd

paper

mathematics

sciences

Avicenna

poetry

The Book of Lords

The Book of Kings

Rabe'a of Qozdar

al-Mutanabbi

Rubaiyat of Omar Khayyam

The Tales from 1001 Nights or *The Arabian Nights*

Sadi

proverbs

Rumi

Sufism

historians

Dome of the Rock

kibla

mosques

Mosque of Samarra

mihrab

minaret

mosque at *Córdoba*

palace of Ukhaidir

Alhambra

mimbar

rugs

arabesques

figurative representations

Tabriz and Herat schools of painting

III. Mapwork

Map 7.1. The Middle East in the Time of Muhammad

What challenges were the Roman (Byzantine) and Sassanian Empires facing at the time of Muhammad? How are their territories transformed in the centuries after his death?

Why are Mecca and Medina important in the life story of Muhammad? What was the original name of this city? Why was it changed?

Who were the Bedouins? Where did they live on the Arabian peninsula? Into which Bedouin tribe was Muhammad born?

Where did Muhammad receive his recitations from Gabriel?

Map 7.2 The Expansion of Islam

What is *jihad*? Consider all possible interpretations of this Arabic word. How does this concept explain Islamic expansion?

Did Muhammad himself ever engage in *jihad*? Why?

What hindered Islamic expansion in the west at Poiters (Tours) and in the east at Constantinople?

Map 7.3. The Abbasid Caliphate at the Height of its Power

How was power transferred between the Ummayad and the Abbasid dynasties? Where did each caliphate locate its capital?

What is a caliph? What controversy surrounded this office after the death of Muhammad?

Who were the Seljuk Turks? How did the Fatimids contribute to their rise to power?

Map 7.4. The Turkish Occupation of Anatolia

What happened in 1071 that led to a crisis in the Byzantine Empire? How did this lead to the Crusades?

Why were the powers in Europe eager to embark on the crusades? Was Jerusalem or Constantinople their main concern? Why?

What was the role of Saladin in these Islamic-Christian conflicts?

IV. Datework

Chapter Timeline: From the birth of Muhammad to the fall of Constantinople to the Ottoman Turks

Why does the Islamic calendar begin not with the birth of the Prophet, but with his flight to Medina? What is the Arabic word for this event?

When scholars consider the spread of Islam as a religious faith into Spain and northwestern India (and elsewhere), what political and cultural changes must also be considered important?

Under whose leadership do the Mongols destroy Baghdad?

Chronology. Islam: The First Millennium

Compare this chronology with the maps in this chapter (7.1 through 7.4 above), and as you consider the importance of each event on this chronology, locate the following: Mecca and Medina, Cairo, the northern boundary of Islamic Spain, Baghdad, Cairo, Constantinople.

What schism within Islam did the election of Ali to the caliphate initiate?

How many crusades were there? Why were they unsuccessful in the end?

Were the Seljuk Turks Muslims? Were the Mongols?

V. Primary Sourcework

Islamic Primary Sources:

The Koran and the Spread of the Muslim Faith from the Koran: Chapter 47, "Muhammad, Revealed at Medina"

In addition to the Koran, in what other sacred work are the sayings of Muhammad to be found?

Why was this Paradise attractive to the original Bedouin tribes?

According to this passage, what justifies the spread of Islam? What motivates believers?

Why did Muhammad conquer Mecca, the city of his birth? How did he accomplish this?

A Pilgimage to Mecca: Ibn Jubayr, *Travels*

What was the original meaning of sacred stones among the Bedouins?

What is the Ka'aba? Where did it come from, and what was its original purpose? How did Muhammad transform it?

Why is an understanding of the "five pillars" central to a comprehension of Islam? What are the other four pillars?

The Murder of Ja'far al-Barmaki: al-Mas'udi, *The Meadows of Gold: The Fall of the Barmakids*

To which of the dynasties did Harun al-Rashid belong? What accusations about the lifestyle of this dynasty's caliphs are reflected here?

What was the meaning of Harun's epithet "al-Rashid"? How does this name apply here?

What elements of folk tale do you perceive here? How does this affect your opinion of the historicity of this narrative?

What is the importance of *The Meadows of Gold* for the history of Islamic literature?

The Crusades in Muslim Eyes: Usamah, *Book of Reflections*

The Crusaders were often collectively termed "Franks" after the region of France. Where (in addition to France) did crusaders actually come from? At whose instigation did they come to the Middle East?

Why was Usamah concerned about the direction of his prayer? Why was the Frankish crusader? What is a *qiblah*?

On what grounds does Usamah base his superiority to the Franks?

What evidence do you see here that the Frankish Knight Usamah calls "King Fulk" felt superior to Usamah in turn?

Given this mutual feeling, why did the two men form a close friendship? Or did they?

A Consumer's Guide to the Ideal Slave: A Father's Instructions to His Son

From what regions and populations did Muslims acquire slaves? Why?

Would this document have seemed remarkable to a Greek or Roman of ancient times? Given what you know about these societies from Chapters Four and Five, why or why not?

What uses does Kai Ka'us have in mind for slaves? What "types" does he advise purchasing for each respective purpose?

What evidence do you see here that although slaves were evaluated like products in the market, some would be destined for humane treatment in the household?

Arabic Literature:

Love for a Camel: The Ode of Tarafah

Compare the concern of the poet Tarafah to the concerns of the consumer above (in A Consumer's Guide to the Ideal Slave). Why is careful attention given to physiognomy in both passages?

What role did the camel play in Arabic society? What effect did its presence have on the economy?

Is the "singing-wench"at all similar to the author's camel? Why might the audience be invited to make such a comparison?

The Tale of Shahrazad: *The Arabian Nights*

What evidence do you see here that Shahrazad strove to make her stories as elaborate as possible, in order to intrigue her captor? What decorative elements does she weave in? What erotic ones?

How is the Arabic practice of polygyny reflected in this tale?

Compare this passage to the passage from the Koran above. Is the magical place Shahrazad describes anything like the Islamic paradise?

With what audience have these tales been most popular? Why?

Be Thankful for Small Favors: Sadi, *The Rose Garden, Stories 7 and 8*

For what "small favor" should the slave in the story be grateful? What moral lesson does this impart to Sadi's audience?

Is the philosopher's cure for the slave's fears compassionate? Is it wise?

Why does Nushirvan disregard the advice of his courtiers? What is his reward?

Why is *The Rose Garden* an apt title for Sadi's collection of stories studded with proverbs?

Sufi Primary Source:

The Passions of a Sufi Mystic: Rumi, *Call to the Dance*

What evidence do you see here that the goals and beliefs of Sufism contrasted with those of orthodox Islam?

Consider this passage in light of the concept of *nirvana* from Chapter Two. Can Indian and Sufi mysticism be compared? How?

Although the dervishes are not mentioned here, how are their rituals implicitly present?

According to this excerpt, what was the definition of a human being according to Sufism?

VI. Artwork

Islamic Shrine:

The Ka'aba in Mecca

How did the Ka'aba become a symbol of Islamic monotheism? What was its original purpose?

Are the other "five pillars" of Islam meant to be performed once in a lifetime? How do each of those practices strengthen the idea of the "wheel" of Islam or the community of believers (*umma*)?

Islamic Art:

Muhammad and the Sacred Stone

What was the name given to the supreme deity represented by this sacred stone? Is this name retained within Islam?

Why did Muhammad "cleanse" the Ka'aba of its polytheistic deities, rather than destroy it?

Why would a work of art such as this be deemed inappropriate for adornment of a mosque? What is its actual origin?

The Destruction of Baghdad by the Mongols

How has the painter of this fourteenth-century miniature distinguished Mongols from Abbasids?

How did the Mongols modify their tactics of conquest after they became established in the Arabic world?

Arab Merchants in a Caravan

Why were Muslims, along with Jews and Christians, known as a "People of the Book"?

What goods travelled the caravan routes across the Arabian peninsula? How does this flourishing trade contribute to urbanization in the Arab empire? Do all classes of people profit?

What were the "fleets of the desert?"

Photograph of Tangier today:

A Tangier Spice Market

How did the Arabic spice trade lead to the development of banking techniques, the use of currency, and systems of credit? What other goods were involved?

Islamic Art and Architecture:

Painting from the "Story of the Shahs"

What East Asian influences do you see in this Islamic painting?

Why do these artistic changes occur after the thirteenth century?

The Temple Mount at Jerusalem

Why is the Dome of the Rock a sacred site to Judaism, Christianity, and Islam?

Identify the minaret of the Dome of the Rock mosque. What was the purpose of the minaret structure? The *kibla*? The *mihrab*?

An Entrance Portal

Why are geometric designs characteristic of Islamic art? What craft especially disseminated the artistic use of arabesques?

The word "mosque" in Arabic means "the place where a man prostrates himself to pray." Why is this an appropriate name for a place of Islamic worship? What does the Arabic word "Islam" mean?

Why would the mosaics adorning mosques begin with austerity and evolve into more free use of color? What similarity do you see between this evolution and contemporary changes in painting?

The Mosque at Córdoba

How has the architect of this mosque created a paradox between mass and lightness in his structure? What might be the meaning of such a paradox?

When did Islam first encompass Spain? By what route was this achieved?

The Alhambra in Granada

The Caliph for whom this palace was built is said to have desired it to be an earthly expression of Paradise. How was this achieved?

What features of Islamic architecture would be an important influence on European architecture of the Middle Ages? Are any of these features present here?

VII. Identifying Important Concepts Behind the Conclusion

The Conclusion to this chapter recalls the following key ideas:

1. Rise and fall of the Arab empire
2. Muhammad and the principles of Islam
3. Islamic legacy

Review these general concepts before moving on to the next chapter.

Chapter Eight: Early Civilizations in Africa

I. Outlining the Chapter

The Land

Emergence of Civilization
- Kush
- Axum, Son of Saba
- Sahara and Its Environs
- East Africa, Land of Zanj
- South Africa

Coming of Islam
- Kingdom of Ethiopia: A Christian Island in a Muslim Sea

East Africa and the Indian Ocean Trade

State Building in West Africa
- Ghana
- Mali
- Government and Kingship in West Africa

States and Stateless Societies in Southern Africa
- Zimbabwe

Aspects of African Society
- Urban Life
- Family, Village, and Women
  - Role of Women
  - Slavery

Religious Beliefs in Traditional Africa

African Culture
- Painting and Sculpture
- Music
- Architecture
- Literature

Conclusion

II. Terms and Persons To Know

diverse geographical zones

Sahara, grassland, and Congo

Kush or Nubia

Egypt

Meroë

Axum

Saba

Coptic Christianity

Ethiopia

savannahs

dessication

trans-Sahara trade

Berbers

Iron Age

Nok

Periplus

Zanj

Bantu-speaking peoples

Indian Ocean trade

Malay

Khoisan-speaking peoples

Arab conquest of Africa

Cairo

Byzantine empire

Axum decline

Muslim Adal

Zagwe dynasty

Solomonids

commercial centers

Mombasa, Pemba, Zanzibar, and Kilwa

Al-Mas'udi

Swahili

Ghana

gold

Mali

Songhai, Kanem-Bornu and Hausa

Timbuktu

mansa

Mansa Musa

hereditary monarchy

Islam

stateless societies

Zaire River valley

Luba

Kongo

Zimbabwe

Great Zimbabwe

San

written records

villages

clans

kingship

Ibn Battuta

lineage groups

"big man"

role of women

matrilinear lineage

slavery

creator god

pantheon

ancestors

sasa

zamani

conversion to Islam

"art:" religious vs. aesthetic purpose

rock paintings

carving and sculpture

dance

music

rhythmic pattern

"talking drum"

"call and response"

architecture

pyramids

stelae

rock churches

use of stone

literature

oral traditions

bards

Son-Jara

III. Mapwork

Map 8.1. Ancient Africa

In what region of the continent did hominids first appear?

What influence did the kingdom of Saba (Sabaea on this map) have on Axum?

Why was iron such an important commodity? What were its uses in Africa, and when and how did it arrive? To which societies did it give a decisive military advantage?

Locate and briefly describe these diverse geographical zones on the continent: desert, grassland, tropical jungles, savannah. Do your descriptions fit the pattern of Stone Age agriculture indicated here? Locate and briefly explain the importance of these waters: the Red Sea, the Nile, Congo River, Zambezi River.

Map 8.2. Ancient Ethiopia and Nubia

By what process did Ethiopia become a Christian Kingdom? What is "Coptic" Christianity?

What was the ancient name of Ethiopia? By what other name was Nubia known?

Why would Ethiopia later be termed "a Christian Island in a Muslim sea?"

Why were relations between Ethiopia and Nubia competitive?

Map 8.3. Trans-Saharan Trade Routes

Why was trans-Saharan trade so crucial to the cultural development of Africa? What goods were transported? What societies participated?

Map 8.4. The Emergence of States in Africa

Concerning the West African kingdoms, what economic structures and principles of kingship supported these societies?

Where are the Swahili cultures located on this map? What were the salient characteristics of these states?

How did Kongo influence early stereotypes about the whole of Africa?

IV. Datework

Chapter Timeline: From the First Agricultural Settlements to the Kingdom of Zimbabwe

What was the Saharan region like in the era previous to its dessication? What evidence demonstrates today that the region was once fertile? Where is this evidence located on Map 8.1 (Ancient Africa)?

Why would the trans-Saharan trade routes become an important alternative to the Mediterranean sea routes for merchants transporting goods between the Far or Middle East and Europe?

Who were the Kushites? What was their relationship with Egypt?

What were the first states to arise in West Africa?

Chronology: Early Africa

Although Egypt is located on the African continent, what historical factors place it in Chapter One with the first Mesopotamian empires? What influence did Egypt have on African peoples to the south and to the west?

Outline the role of the Berbers in African history. What is their role in the development of trade? In the adoption of Islam?

What distinguishes the Bantu from other peoples in East Africa? Who are the Malays? Who built the Great Zimbabwe, and what was its purpose?

V. Primary Sourcework

Primary Sources on Africa:

The Conquest of Kush: An Axumite King Proclaims His Victory

Why is the author careful to distinguish between stone towns and straw villages?

What religious faith does this Axumite king claim supported him in his victories?

Beyond the Pillars of Hercules: Herodotus, *History of the Persian Wars*

Why does Herodotus reproduce this account when he does not believe it himself? Why are we indebted to him for doing so?

Trace the journey of these Phoenicians on Map 8.1. Why did this journey take two years?

The Coast of Zanj: Al-Mas'udi in East Africa

Why does Al-Mas'udi admire the people of Zanj?

What signs do you see in his text that the author is writing for an upper-class Muslim audience? How does this influence what he reports?

A Description of a Ghanaian Capital: Al-Bakri's Description of Ghana

Why does al-Bakri refer to the religious images of the royal Ghanaian kings as "idols"?

What evidence does the author give that followers of traditional religion and Islam lived peacefully together? What does the author call the traditional religion? Why?

How did accounts like this lead outsiders to refer to the West African kingdoms collectively as "The Gold Coast"?

The Kingdom of Borno: Leo Africanus, *The History and Description of Africa*

What was more valuable in Borno, slaves or horses? Why?

What characteristics led Leo Africanus to term this king "puissant"?

What factors led him to conclude that "They embrace no religion at all...." Is he correct? Why might he have failed to consider traditional rituals as "religion"?

Women and Islam in North Africa: Leo Africanus, *The History and Description of Africa*

What is Leo Africanus describing when he refers to "certain masks"? What was their purpose?

Where was this custom of female dress adopted in Africa? What evidence do you see here for the blending of traditional custom with outside influences?

A Chinese View of Africa: Chau Ju-kua on East Africa

What are the "dead fish" Chau Ju-kua describes? How do you know?

What particular practices of the "sorcerers" have been reported to this Chinese author? Who were his informants? Why would he learn especially of the sorcerers illegal "charms" over ships?

Why would a thirteenth-century Chinese scholar be especially interested in the eastern coast of Africa as he compiled a treatise on geography? To what uses might his geography be put?

A West African Oral Tradition: The Epic of Son-Jara

Why were bards so important in West African culture?

How did they support with their craft the legitimacy of West African kings?

VI. Artwork

African Art:

The Pyramids at Meroë

As the caption (and chapter narrative) indicates, Kush imported certain cultural elements (e.g., the pyramid) from Egypt, yet transformed these elements to suit their unique society. How is this pattern of adoption tempered by transformation also characteristic of Africa's acceptance of Islam? Of Christianity?

The influence of Egypt on Kush is evident; how was Egypt influenced by Kush in return?

The Stele at Axum

Why did Axumite rulers erect such stelae? How does this purpose differ from the use of stelae by rulers in Mesopotamia? (See, e.g., the stele of Hammurabi in Chapter One.)

Rock Paintings of the Sahara

How might these paintings be compared to the Paleolithic cave paintings discussed and depicted in Chapter One? Are the artistic concerns similar? The subjects? The motivation for the artworks?

What happened to the flourishing culture that produced these artworks?

Mansa Musa

Why would Mansa Musa's gold-spending depreciate the value of gold?

How did the King of Mali gain so much wealth? How was his homeland's location on the trans-Saharan trade routes paramount to his economic success?

Great Zimbabwe

In southern Africa, building in stone was a mark of status. What were the materials used for buildings of lesser importance?

What statement about the rulers of Zimbabwe do these walls make? How must they have been constructed, if no mortar was used? Why does this make this structure even more impressive?

The City of Timbuktu

What economic and political factors led Timbuktu to change from a simple desert oasis to a prosperous and scholarly city?

To which of the West African Kingdoms did Timbuktu belong? What other commercial centers vied with it?

Nok Pottery Head

For what religious rituals might this terra-cotta sculpture have been created?

What were the important beliefs about ancestors in traditional African religion?

African Metalwork, Benin

Why might this sculpture be seen as evidence for matrilineal lineage patterns in Benin?

Consider this bronze sculpture in relation to the excerpt from the Epic of Son-Jara that closes this chapter. How do both attest to the importance of the Queen Mother in African societies?

A Coptic Church in Ethiopia

How was this building constructed? Why does it have this particular shape?

What statement did this church make in contrast to the religious practices of Ethiopia's neighbors?

Why did Coptic, and not Roman Catholic or Greek Orthodox Christianity become the religion of Ethiopia?

The Mosque at Jenne, Mali

Identify the typical mosque features of minaret, dome, and *kibla* wall in the Mosque at Jenne. What features make this building uniquely African?

Which cultures of Africa represent the most prominent influence of Islam?

VII. Identifying Important Concepts Behind the Conclusion

The Conclusion to this chapter recalls the following key ideas:

1. African contributions to world civilizations

2. Trade and consequent transformation of the continent

Review these general concepts, especially in regard to Islamic and Traditional Africa, and the major African states and stateless societies, before moving on to the next chapter.

Chapter Nine: The Expansion of Civilization in Southern Asia

I. Outlining the Chapter

India from the Mauryas to the Mughals

Kushan Kingdom: Linchpin of the Silk Road
- Gupta Dynasty
  - Feudalism, Indian Style
  - Buddhism at Bay
- Islam on the March
  - Importing the Islamic Model
  - Islam and Indian Society
- Economy and Daily Life
- The Wonder of Indian Culture
  - Art and Architecture
  - Literature

Golden Region: Early Southeast Asia
- Beginnings of Civilization
  - Early Contacts with India
- Formation of States
  - Angkor and Other Mainland States
  - Malay World
  - Indian Model in Southeast Asia
- Spices and Paddy Fields: The Economy of Southeast Asia
- Daily Life
- World of the Spirits: Religious Belief
- Cultural World of Southeast Asia

Conclusion

II. Terms and Persons To Know

Mauryan dynasty

Kushan state

Silk Road

Roman trade with the East

Kanishka

Gupta dynasty

Chandragupta, Samadragupta and Chandragupta II

Harsa

feudal system

vassals

devaraja

Theravada

Mahayana

bodhisattva

Avalokitesvara

decline of Buddhism in India

bhakti

Islam

Mahmud of Ghazni

Delhi sultanate

Rajputs

Mongols

Ghengis Khan

Tughluq dynasty

Tamerlane

chakravartin

Hindus and Muslims

purdah

sati

Sikhism

Nanak

non-Hindus and the caste system

commerce and trade

caves of Ajanta

Hindu rock temples

Kailasantha at Ellora

Elephanta

Mamallapuram

temple sculpture

Sun Temple at Konarak

Khajuraho

gopuras

Cola bronzes

rasa

Sanskrit poetry

Kalidasa

Sanskrit plays

Sanskrit prose

Dandin

music

nada

raga

Southeast Asia

migrations

geographical features

Malayo-Polynesians

Indian influence

Funan

Angkor

Thai peoples

Burmans

Pagan

Srivijaya

Sailendra

Majapahit

charisma

linga

pirates

Strait of Malacca

class system

Angkor Thom

kampongs

state cult

Theravada Buddhism

Islam

Buddhist temple at Borobudur

the Bayon

Shwedagon Pagoda

Nagarkertagama

wayang

shadow theatre

gamelan music

III. Mapwork

Map 9.1. The Gupta Empire

Why is the era of the Gupta dynasty known as the "classical age" of Indian civilization?

What is the relationship between the former Kushan Empire and the Gupta Empire?

Describe the flourishing of commerce and trade under the Gupta rulers.

What geographical feature limited this empire in the North? In the South? What non-geographical elements prevented further spread of the empire to the south?

Map 9.2. India at the Death of Mahmud of Ghazni

When was the Ghazni empire founded? How is the foundation of this state related to Islamic trade interests in India?

Why was Mahmud of Ghazni given the epithet "sword of Islam"? Who opposed him?

How did the Colas and the Mongols act to limit the extend of this empire?

Map 9.3. The Empire of Tamerlane

How did Tamerlane rise to power?

In what ways were his military tactics comparable to those of Ghengis Khan?

Which ancient empires occupied the area Tamerlane conquered? Which modern countries occupy this area today?

Map 9.4. Southeast Asia in the Thirteenth Century

Who were the enemies of Angkor? How did the Thai contribute to this state's decline?

Where is the Strait of Malacca on this map? Why was it so crucial for trade in Southeast Asia? Which of these states controlled it in the Thirteenth century?

IV. Datework

Chapter Timeline: From the Kushan kingdom to the Invasion of Tamerlane

Why did civilization in Southeast Asia occur nearly two thousand years after the first civilizations in Mesopotamia, India, and China?

What factors limited cultural transmission between communities in this region?

Explain the importance of the Gupta dynasty. How was this successful order achieved within Indian factionalism and conflict?

What effect did Tamerlane have on India? Compare his impact there with the impact of the Monguls on the Arab empire in Chapter Seven.

Why did Buddhism decline in Southeast Asia, but remain an important influence in Southeast Asia?

Chronology: Medieval India

Why did Fa Xian travel to India? How does his purpose attest to the cultural influence between India and China in ancient times?

What features of Indian life did Xuan Zang find notable? For what purpose did he visit India?

Describe the spread of Islam from the arrival of Arab armies to the peak of the Delhi sultanate. Why was Islam attractive to some Indians? Why was it unattractive to others?

Did any of the conquerers or rulers listed here achieve the Indian ideal of *chakravartin*?

Chronology: Early Southeast Asia

What peoples were involved in the Malayo-Polynesian migration? Where did they originate? How far might their migrations have extended?

Explain how the following interact during the rise of states in Southeast Asia: Funan, Angkor, the Burmans. Why do these states decline?

Why is the Majapahit empire still remembered as important in Indonesia today?

What climatological and archaeological conditions make exact dating in this region so difficult? What is the state of the surviving written records?

What influence did India and China have on all of the cultures of Southeast Asia?

V. Primary Sourcework

Indian Primary Sources:

The Good Life in Medieval India: Fa Xian, *The Travels of Fa Xian*

What evidence do you see here for the caste system? What caste did Fa Xian find particularly interesting?

What dietary prohibitions does this passage document? Are these Hindu or Buddhist in origin?

What freedoms in the lives of the common people does Fa Xian find noteworthy? How might these have contrasted with Chinese conditions in the fifth century?

The Education of a Brahmin: Xuan Zang, *Records of Western Countries*

How is Xuan Zang's description of philosophy similar to the original sense of this word as introduced in Chapter Four?

Of what elements does the education of a *brahmin* consist? At what age is he considered ready to undertake an occupation?

What sort of life, according to Xuan Zang, was the most admirable of all? What elements of the author's Buddhist sensibilities are reflected here?

The Islamic Conquest of India: A Muslim Ruler Suppresses Hindu Practices

What was the origin of the Islamic prohibition against alcohol?

Explain how the following played a part in the conflict between Hinduism and Islam in India: monotheism, hierarchy, priests, beef, idolatry, and sexual frankness in art.

Why did the *sudra* find Islam appealing?

How are Ala-ud-din's difficulties similar to those lawmakers faced in this country during the time of Prohibition? Why does the Muslim ruler soften his laws to allow private drinking in the end?

The Practice of Sati: Duarte Barbosa, *On Sati*

What was Barbosa attempting to describe when he noted "three classes of Heathen"?

How is the practice of *sati* evidence of the patriarchal nature of Indian society? How does it demonstrate the severe distinctions drawn between the upper and lower classes?

Why would a widow not be encouraged to live on after her husband? Or to marry again and perhaps have more children?

Was the woman who threw herself on the pyre truly happy and acting of her own free will? What details in Barbosa's account support such a conclusion? Do you believe it?

Untouchables in South India: Duarte Barbosa, *From the Land of Malabar*

What similarity do you see between the behavior of the untouchables in this passage and the passage "The Good Life in Medieval India" above? Why were such alerting actions deemed necessary?

Why was Barbosa's opinion of the Poleas so low?

Whom did Barbosa probably interview in order to learn about the Poleas?

How might this passage, along with the passage on *sati* above, attest to the status of women in Indian society in the medieval era?

An Indian Love Poem: Kalidasa, *The Cloud Messenger*

To whom is the young exile speaking in the first five stanzas? To whom in the final stanza?

Which of the *rasas* is intended in each section of the poem? How does Kalidasa create the meditative quality appropriate for these?

Southeast Asian Primary Sources:

The Kingdom of Angkor: Chau Ju-kua, *Records of Foreign Nations*

How does this document demonstrate both Indian and Chinese influence on religious life in Angkor?

Does this passage attest to Theravada or Mahayana practices in Angkor Thom?

The Legendary Grandeur of Majapahit: Prapanca, *Nagarkertagama*

Why was Prapanca eager to associate Java with India? How does he do this?

How did the prince of Majapahit, although not born into an Indian caste, become known as a *brahmin*?

VI. Artwork

Indian Art:

Mamallapuram Ocean Temple

Describe the architectural differences between free-standing and rock-cut Hindu temples.

How does this temple attest to the polytheistic nature of Hinduism?

What images predominated in the sculptural decoration of Hindu temple walls?

Kutub Minar

How do the mosque on the site of Delhi's largest Hindu temple and the Kutub Minar attest to the initial outcome of the Hindu-Islamic conflict in India? From where did the building materials for these structures come?

Were India's Muslim rulers ever successful in converting the majority of the population to Islam? Was conversion attempted by force or by influence? How did economics play a role?

Art of Sri Lanka:

Rock Paintings at Sigiriya, Sri Lanka

What similarities do you see between these paintings and the Hindu carvings pictured elsewhere in this chapter? Between these paintings and the ancient Indian art depicted in Chapter Two?

Why would Buddhist monks have attempted to destroy all of these images?

Indian Art:

Rock Temple at Ellora

Why does such an architectural monument represent not only Hindu belief, but absolute devotion on the part of the workers?

Who are the most important of the Hindu deities that would be represented here? In spite of such a proliferation of gods, is Hinduism truly polytheistic?

Descent of the Ganges River

How do you see the artistic style known as *horror vacui* (avoidance of empty space) at work here? How does this characteristic contribute to the impact of the relief?

Who was Siva?

Why would this monument have been unacceptable to Muslim eyes?

Sculptural Decorations at Khajuraho

Relate this visual artwork to the principle of erotic *rasa* in Indian literature.

How might this sculpture, which represents the ideal couple or divine lovers in human form, be compared with the Indian and Southeast Asian governmental ideal of *devaraja*?

Southeast Asian Architecture:

Angkor Wat

How does this architectural monument demonstrate the principle of *devaraja* in Angkor?

In what way would such a temple promote the charisma of the king? His status as *brahmin*?

What similarities do you see between this structure and the Hindu temples from India above? Why do such strong similarities exist?

Photograph of Southeast Asia:

Mount Agung in Bali

In what other cultures considered in previous chapters have mountains been considered sacred? Why?

How have the plate tectonics associated with volcanic activity formed the unique geographical features of this region?

Southeast Asian art and architecture:

The Bayon at Angkor

What was the significance of *bodhisattvas* for Buddhism? Was this an important concept for both Theravada and Mahayana strands of this religion? Why or why not?

Who was Jayavarman?

The Temple of Borobudur

Why was Buddhism, and the concept of an "immanent Buddha" attractive to local rulers in Southeast Asia?

What is the purpose of a stupa? What is the Buddhist teaching about the state of Nirvana? (If necessary, review Chapter Two.) Do these concepts differ in Theravada and Mahayana Buddhism? Which of these schools was most attractive in Java?

Why did Buddhism decline on Java in the ninth century?

Followers of the Buddha Borobudur

Why would the artist who carved these relief sculptures have chosen to depict followers of the living Buddha in the costumes of his own time and place (eighth-century Java)? What does such anachronism accomplish?

In which level of the temple of Borobudur (above) would these carvings have been located?

VII. Identifying Important Concepts Behind the Conclusion

The Conclusion to this chapter recalls the following key ideas:

1. Conflicts on the Indian continent between the Mauryan dynasty to the rise of the Mughal dynasty

2. Hinduism, Buddhism, and Islam

3. Southeast Asia

Review these general concepts before moving on to the next chapter.

Chapter Ten
From the Tang to the Mongols: The Flowering of Traditional China

I. Outlining the Chapter

China after the Han

China Reunified: The Sui, The Tang, and the Song
- Political Structures: The Triumph of Confucianism
  - Equal Opportunity in China: The Civil Service Examination
  - Local Government
- Economy and Society
  - A Commercial Revolution?
  - Daily Life in Traditional China

Explosion in Central Asia: The Mongol Empire
- Mongol Rule in China
- Mongol's Place in History

Ming Dynasty
- Ming Hongwu: The People's Emperor
- The Ming Turn Inward

In Search of the Way
- Rise and Decline of Buddhism and Daoism
- Neo-Confucianism: The Investigation of Things

Apogee of Chinese Culture
- Literature
- Art

Conclusion

II. Terms and Persons To Know

collapse of the Han

Cao Cao

"era of the six dynasties"

State Confucianism and philosophical Daoism (introduced in Chapter Three)

"seven sages of the bamboo forest"

Liu Ling

Buddhism

Yang Jian

Sui dynasty

Grand Canal

Sui Yangdi

Korean kingdom of Koguryo

Li Yuan

Tang dynasty

Li Shimin

Xinjiang

Chang'an

Xuanzong

Yang Guifei

Uighurs

Song dynasty

Song Taizu

Jin dynasty

Mongols

Grand council

civil service examination

magistrates

village government

"equal field system"

Wang Anshi

new products

currency and credit

Silk Road

sea trade

"younger brothers"

gentry class

daily life

joint family

Empress Wu Zhao

Ghengis Khan

fire-lance

khanates

Khubilai Khan

Yuan dynasty

Mongol rule of China

Hangzhou

Marco Polo

Zhu Yuanzhang or Ming Hongwu

ordos system

Black Death

Pax Mongolica

Ming dynasty

Yongle

Beijing

Li-jia system

naval expeditions

Zhenghe

Buddhist sects

dharma and *dao*

Buddhism, Daoism, and the state

Manichaeanism

Neo-Confucianism

Zhu Xi

Supreme Ultimate

"investigation of things"

Wang Yangming

"School of Mind"

contrast with Europe

paper

printing

poetry

Du Fu

Li Bo

Su Dongpo

Ma Zhiyuan

theatre

short story

novel

Romance of the Three Kingdoms

Tale of the Marshes

Buddhist cave paintings at Dunhuang

secular painting

nature painting

scroll

calligraphy

monochrome painting

literati artists

Yuan painting styles

porcelain

architecture

III. Mapwork

Map 10.1. China under the Tang

What was the effect on the territory of the Chinese empire during the years of anarchy following the Han? (Review the maps from Chapter Three.)

What dynasties immediately preceded the Tang? What were their contributions to Chinese history? Why did they ultimately fall?

Locate the Grand Canal and the Great Wall on this map. How does each represent an important trend in Chinese history?

Which cities marked here served as capitals for a dynasty? Why did imperial rulers relocate China's capital so many times? What concerns are reflected in each move?

Map 10.2. Chang'an under the Sui and the Tang

Locate Chang'an on Map 10.1 above. Which of the emperors located the imperial residence here?

What architectural and civic techniques did the emperor use to emphasize his royal status?

Does this city reflect Daoist or Confucian principles? Why?

Consider this city plan in light of the first primary source in this chapter, "A Daoist Critique of Confucianism." How do you see the *fa*, *li*, and "jade" visually emphasized in Chang'an?

Would the city itself have served as a reminder to its denizens of the "straight rules"?

Map 10.3. Asia under the Mongols

Consider this map in light of the primary source immediately preceding it, "A Letter to the Pope." How does this map visually reflect the concerns of Innocent IV?

Locate Karakorum on the map. What is the importance of this site for the Mongols? How did its existence distinguish Khubilai Khan from the Mongols tribes he ruled?

Who was Marco Polo? Why was he not believed in Europe?

Why were the Mongols so successful in China and so unsuccessful in their attempts at further expansion?

Map 10.4. The Voyages of Zhenghe

What did Zhenghe accomplish for his Ming emperor on his sea navigations?

Why did Yongle put a stop to them? Is this related to his transposition of the imperial capital from Nanjing to Beijing?

What very important effect did the cessation of such voyages have on Chinese history?

IV. Datework

Chapter Timeline: China from the Collapse of the Han to the Yuan Dynasty

What conflicts plagued Chinese society in the era immediately falling the fall of the Han dynasty?

What are some of the major artistic differences in painting and literature betwen the Tang, Song, and Yuan dynasties?

Who built the Grand Canal? Why? Which ruler made it still longer? Why?

Under whose leadership do the voyages of Zhenge occur?

Who first gave the Mongols gunpowder? What effect would this have on Chinese history?

The printing process in Europe is a 15th-century phenomenon. When is printing invented in China? What was the Chinese process like?

Chronology: Medieval China

From where did China import Buddhism? Why did Hinduism not become influential in China as well? How did Buddhism interact with the local traditions of Daoism and Confucianism?

Who founded the Song dynasty? What reforms were attempted by Wang Anshi late in this dynasty's reign? How are the issues his reforms addressed related to the collapse of the Song?

Who was Khubilai Khan? Who followed him in his reign? Why was the Yuan dynasty relatively short-lived?

What impact did the Mongols have on China? How did China influence the Mongols?

What did the first Ming emperor call himself? For what achievements are he and his son Yongle remembered?

V. Primary Sourcework

Chinese Primary Sources:

A Daoist Critique of Confucianism: The Biography of a Great Man

Is the author's final question a serious one? What difference is there between the Confucian "gentleman" described here and lice that inhabit trouser legs? What similiarity does he mean us to see?

Why is the Daoist author so critical of Confucianism?

What major changes would external criticisms from both Daoism and Buddhism cause within State Confucianism?

The Good Life in the High Tang: Du Fu, *A Poem*

How did the poetry of Du Fu contrast with that of Li Bo? How do the two together represent the literary concerns of Tang poets?

How is Du Fu's reader to distinguish his distaste for this imperial display? Might this poem not be read as an expression of admiration? Why? Why would the author make the distinction fairly subtle?

See Map 10.2 above. Where might this festival have taken place within Chang'an?

This poem seems to spring from the poet's direct experience of an imperial gala. Why would Du Fu have been present at this festival? Do his acceptance of the invitation and his consequent scornful poem create a paradox? Why or why not?

The Saintly Miss Wu: Hung Mai, *A Song Family Saga*

What similarities do you see between the view of widows expressed here and the ancient Indian practice of *sati*? (Review Chapter Two.)

Why did unmarried persons have little voice in Chinese village life under the clan and council system?

How did Miss Wu express her filial piety? Why would she represent the "perfect woman" in medieval Chinese society?

What moral lesson are we to conclude from Miss Wu's miraculous salvation? For whom is this message especially intended?

A Letter to the Pope: A Letter from Kuyuk Khan to Pope Innocent IV

Why (aside from its obvious refusal to heed the pope's request) would Kuyuk Khan's reply have displeased Innocent IV?

What beliefs on the part of the Khan are reflected here? How does he justify his own power?

What specifically has displeased Pope Innocent IV? How does the Khan justify these acts? Under what dynasty were these letters exchanged?

What does the Khan make of the Pope's unique position within the Roman Catholic Church? Does he understand it?

How Khubilai Khan Chooses His Consorts: Marco Polo, *The Travels of Marco Polo*

What is the distinction between a legitimate wife and a concubine? Could both provide an heir to the Chinese throne? Why would this be both a practical and a dangerous plan for successors?

How does the royal household, in this respect, reflect family life in everyday China?

Is the Khan's selection of consorts a beauty contest? A form of exacting tribute from conquered peoples? Both? What similarities do you see between this passage from Marco Polo and the Islamic guidelines for buying a slave from Chapter Seven?

The Way of the Great Buddha

What similarities to philosophical Daoism do you perceive here? Why does the document contain them?

Can one define the Buddhist concept of Nirvana? The Chinese concept of the Dao? Why did Shen-Hui try?

Why were both Buddhism and Daoism rejected as dangerous by the Chinese state under the Tang?

The Neo-Confucian View of the Universe: Shao Yung, *Supreme Principles Governing the World*

What was new about Neo-Confucianism? How do the principles of *yin* and *yang* provide continuity and represent this evolution?

In response to what pressures did Neo-Confucianism develop?

What were the contributions of Zhu Xi and Wang Yangming to this movement?

What is the Supreme (or Great) Ultimate? What is the "investigation" considered here?

Two Tang Poets: Li Bo, *Night Thoughts* and *Drinking Alone in Moonlight*, and Du Fu, *Spring Prospect*

Which of these poets reflects concerns of state? Which reflects private concerns? Which would be more closely associated with Daoism?

Why might the first of Li Bo's poems have become popular as a school text, while the second example has not?

What were the principles of organization and aesthetic beauty in this age of Chinese poetry?

A Battle to the Death: *Tale of the Marshes*

Why would such an account have appealed more to common than to imperial or aristocratic tastes?

How does this novel reflect the mood of the Chinese people under the Yuan dynasty?

Do you find this passage believable? Why might realism have been irrelevant to its original audience?

VI. Artwork

Chinese Art:

The Buddhist Pilgrim Xuan Zang

Under which dynasty did Xuan Zang leave China to travel to India?

Was he a missionary or a pilgrim? What is the distinction between the two?

Why did this devout Buddhist have such zeal to visit India?

Photograph of the Silk Road:

The Heavenly Mountains

What were the other possible routes for the Silk Road? Why were they less attractive than the route along the Heavenly Mountains?

Consider this photograph along with the first artwork in this chapter, "The Buddhist Pilgrim Xuan Zang." How was that artwork a product of the Silk Road and its trials?

How did the Silk Road culturally and ecnomically benefit China?

ChineseArt:

Spring Festival on the River

How was scroll art related to the principles and values of Daoism?

Who is the expected audience for such a painting? What was the intended result upon the viewer?

Why would the artist have been so meticulous in identifying each class of society from the others? Identify the various classes. Are women and children present here? How does their treatment reflect their roles in medieval Chinese society?

Photograph of the Great Wall:

The Great Wall of China

Why is this portion of the Great Wall mistakenly believed to be of such great antiquity? (See Chapter Three.) Which of the Ming emperors actually ordered the work seen in this photograph?

What other civic improvement projects were undertaken by the Ming?

How does the rise of the Ming dynasty represent a radical break with the immediate past in Chinese tradition?

Making Paper

What were some of the many purposes of paper among the Chinese in the medieval period? Did the common person use this commodity?

What were the first Chinese literary masterworks to be produced on paper?

How did this printing process work? How did the structure of the Chinese language affect this procedure?

Longmen Caves Buddhist Sculpture

Why can the Silk Road be fairly termed "an avenue for ideas as well as trade"? Were all these imported ideas religious ones?

How do these sculptures visually express the values of Tang, as opposed to Song, art?

Why did many of the emperors of China, unlike Gaozong, reject Buddhism?

A Mountain Scene

Why are the human beings in this painting so small? Why are human works (e.g., the bridge and temple) also so diminutive? What Daoist principles are expressed in such proportions?

As the chapter narrative states of Daoist painters, "Rather than depicting the actual realistic shape of a specific mountain, they tried to portray the idea of "mountain." What is the difference?

Why were empty spaces left in some Daoist paintings? What teaching is reflected in that technique?

Under what dynasty did Fan K'uan produce this painting?

Li Bo Chanting a Poem

How did Tang painting react to the styles of painters under the Song? What political motivations caused this reaction?

What influence has the art of calligraphy had upon Liang Kai?

Why did Li Bo become so admired after his death? How did the legend about his death reflect his poetic concerns?

The Temple of Heaven

Why did Yongle move the imperial capital from Nanjing to Beijing?

How is the emperor's role in state ritual reflected here?

Does innovation or continuity characterize Chinese architecture in the medieval period? Why?

VII. Identifying Important Concepts Behind the Conclusion

The Conclusion to this chapter recalls the following key ideas:

1. Sucession of dynasties from the end of the Han to the Ming
2. Civil, agrarian, governmental, and commercial patterns
3. Cultural and artistic achievements

Review these general concepts before moving on to the next chapter.

Chapter Eleven
The East Asian Rimlands: Early Japan, Korea, and Vietnam

I. Outlining the Chapter

Japan: Land of the Rising Sun
- A Gift from the Gods: Prehistoric Japan
- Rise of the Japanese State
  - Emulating the Chinese Model
  - Nara and Heian Periods
  - Kamakura Shogunate and After
  - Daily Life
- In Search of the Pure Land: Religion in Early Japan
- Sources of Traditional Japanese Culture
  - Literature
  - Art and Architecture
- Japan and the Chinese Model

Korea
- Three Kingdoms
- Unification
- Under the Mongols

Vietnam: The Smaller Dragon
- Rise of the Great Viet
  - Chinese Legacy
- Society and Family Life

Conclusion

II. Terms and Persons To Know

four islands of Japan

geography and environment

cultural and racial homogeneity

birth of Japan

Amaterasu

Jomon peoples

Yayoi culture

"divine warrior"

uji

Yamato state

Shotoku Taishi

missions to the Tang court

seventeen-article constitution

Taika reforms

Buddhism

Shinto

epidemics

Fujiwara

Nara

"son of Heaven"

civil service examinations

Heian

shoen system

samurai

Bushido

Minamoto Yoritomo

bakufu

shogun

Kamakura shogunate

Mongols

Khubilai Khan

kamikaze

Ashikaga shogunate

daimyo

Onin War

Kyoto

wet rice

trade

manufacturing

class distinctions

court life

Murasaki Shikibu

common people

genin

eta

tatami

women

kami

ancestral spirits

nature

Ise

Pure Land

Zen

satori

zazen

haniwa

hybrid writing system

poetry

traditional thirty-one syllables

haiku

female prose

The Tale of Genji

Kamakura novels

The Tale of the Heike

No drama

Chinese architectural forms

Heian and Kamakura hand scrolls

"guardian king" sculptures

Muramachi art

Zen influence

gardens

Golden Pavilion

Ryoanji Temple

tea ceremony

isolation

Chinese influence

Korean peninsula

farming

Shang founder?

Chosun

Pyongyang

Han dynasty

Koguryo

Paekche

Silla

Japanese colonies

Buddhism

civil war

Koryo dynasty

Taejo

"great wall"

chonmin

Tripitaka

bakufu elements

Mongols

Yi Song-gye

Yi dynasty

Vietnam

Red River delta

Viets

Qin dynasty

Han dynasty

Trung sisters

sinification

Annam

Chinese influence

Buddhist, Daoist, and Confucian themes

Dai Viet

Champa

Thang Long

"March to the South"

Song dynasty

Mongols

Ming dynasty

Chinese influence on government, art, architecture and literature

Mandate of Heaven

civil service examination

official hierarchy

"smaller dragon"

monarch

poetry

Chu Nom

class system

family

women

III. Mapwork

Map 11.1. Japan, China, and Korea, 600-800

What were the purposes of the Japanese embassies? To which of the Chinese dynasties were they sent?

Which Japanese emperor initiated these missions? Why?

What geographical factors result in separate destinies, but mutual awareness, between Japan, Korea, and Vietnam?

Why were the rulers of all three known in medieval China as "little brothers" of the Chinese emperor?

Map 11.2. Early Japan

What role does the region near Kyoto play in early Japanese history? The Kamakuran peninsula?

What prevented the success of the Mongol invasion of Japan in 1281? Where did the Mongol fleet land?

Where is Korea on this map?

IV. Datework

Chapter Timeline: Jimmu's migration to Central Japan to the Vietnamese Conquest of Champa

What was the influence of the Tang on Japan? Of the Han on Korea and Vietnam? How did the Mongols affect all three lands? Did the khans succeed in holding all three?

Why is an understanding of Chinese history a necessary prerequisite for comprehending the histories and cultures of Japan, Korea, and Vietnam? How is your answer reflected on this timeline?

Chronology: The Formation of the Japanese State

Briefly describe the following: the Taika reforms, the Nara and Heian periods, the Kamakura shogunate, and the Onin wars.

Why did Japanese embassies to China stop in the Heian period?

How did Shotoku Taishi contribute to the centralization of the Japanese governmen? How did Minamoto Yoritomo?

Why is Murasaki Shikibu important to the artistic history of Japan?

Chronology: Early Korea and Vietnam

Why were the Trung sisters able to succeed with their revolt against the Han in Vietnam?

Explain the importance of Annam to the Chinese emperors. Do you perceive any similarity between this goal and the Vietnamese "March to the South"?

Which of the three kingdoms of Korea emerges as dominant over the others?

V. Primary Sourcework

Japanese Primary Sources:

The Eastern Expedition of Emperor Jimmu: *The Chronicles of Japan*

What was the relationship between the founder of the Japanese imperial family and the gods of Japan? Where did Amaterasu come from?

Is this belief in a divine origin of the emperor prevalent in Japan today?

How are the realities of Japanese geography reflected here?

How does this passage document the historical tensions between forces of centralization and decentralization in the government of Japan?

The Seventeen-Article Constitution: *The Chronicles of Japan*

Consider this document alongside Map 11.1. How did the embassies of Shotoku Taishi lead to the promulgation of this constitution in Japan?

What evidence does this document provide about life in the Yamato state?

According to this passage, what Chinese influences were prevalent in this state?

Why is Shinto not mentioned here?

Japan's Warrior Class: *The Way of the Samurai*

Why does the samurai feel the need to justify his way of life? Do you see any relation between his questioning and the traditional Chinese view of the merchans class? How does the samurai resemble a merchant class? How is he very different?

Who are the three classes? How does the samurai relate to them?

What evidence does this document provide for the spiritual, not merely martial, values of the samurai?

Why does the author mention "the Way" in the final paragraph? What Chinese philosophy has been influential here?

Do you detect Buddhist or Confucianist values in this document? How were these "imports" to Japan important in Japanese morals, institutions, and aesthetics?

The Seduction of the Akashi Lady: *The Tale of Genji*

Who is the author of this novel? How is its authorship a reflection of Japanese literate society? Is this a reflection of the role of women in Japanese society at large? Or of the role of women at court?

Is the emphasis in this passage on action, or on emotion? Does this excerpt faithfully reflect the novel as a whole in this respect?

What evidence do you see here that has led scholars to call this work "the first psychological novel"?

What has Genji done? Does his wife mind? Can we tell from her letter? How does her response affect Genji?

Life in the Land of Wa: *History of the Wei Dynasty*

Why did the Chinese refer to Japan as the "land of *Wa*"?

Why, considering Japanese laws concerning divorce, might this Chinese author have noticed that in Japan, "Women are chaste and not given to jealousy. They do not engage in thievery...."?

What evidence does this document provide for third-century Japanese agricultural life, trade, and social institutions and practices?

A Lament of the Common Man: *Manyoshu*

Why is it extremely unlikely that a poor man actually write this poem? What was the author's purpose in "creating" the voice of a lower class person?

How is the mood of this poem similar to the traditional examples given within the chapter narrative?

To which class would the person speaking in this poem have belonged?

A Sample of Linked Verse: *The Three Poets at Minase*

What is "linked verse"? How does it differ from earlier traditional Japanese poetic form?

How have the ideas of Daoism and Zen been influential upon this poem?

How would this poem have been written down? How do the Chinese and Japanese languages and writing systems differ?

Korean Primary Source:

The Flower Garden Scripture: An Eighth-Century Buddhist Scripture

Which Buddhist sect has influenced Master Yongi of Hwangyong? How does the importance of ritual in the text and the author's emphasis on bodhisattvas determine your answer?

How could copying lead to salvation?

What similarities do you see between these copying directives and the physical requirements for proper hand scroll and tea ceremony performance?

Vietnamese Primary Source:

The Chinese Conquest of Vietnam: *The Huai Nan Tzu*

Who were the Viet? How were they traditionally viewed by the Chinese? Why?

What factors enabled the Vietnamese to ultimately defeat the larger and better-equipped Chinese forces?

Why had the Chinese invaded the Red River delta?

VI. Artwork

Japanese Art and Architecture:

Samurai

In what ways was the samurai warrior similar to a medieval knight in Europe? How was he different?

How does the *shoen* system result in the creation of these military retainers?

What was *bushido*? How does the rise of the samurai reflect the failure of the Taika reforms of Emperor Shotoku Taishi?

The Burning of the Palace

What was the purpose of the hand scroll? How does this relate to the Chinese Daoist paintings discussed in Chapter Ten?

How were Heian hand scrolls different from Kamakuran ones? How are these differences reflected here?

Scene of Urban Life

What is a daimyo? How was this role important in Japanese village life? What did this Japanese word mean?

Locate Edo on Map 11.2. What factors led to the rise of this city within a predominantly agrarian country?

Is this a hand scroll? How is it similar to the previous art work, "The Burning of the Palace"? Who would have been the intended audience for this painting?

Portrait of a Zen Master

Why were spiritual and mental intensity important values within Zen Buddhism?

What teaching about *satori* do these values, and this painting, reflect?

How is the concept of *satori* related to the Indian, and Chinese, concept of Nirvana?

When does realism, or even gruesome realism, become dominant in Japanese portraiture? Why? What had characterized earlier portrait styles?

Guardian Kings

Explain the different aesthetic values of Heian and Kamakuran art.

Such statues once graced Buddhist shrines. Did such figures adorn Shinto shrines? How were Shinto beliefs and places of worship different?

How are the different appearances of Buddhist and Shinto sites expressive of their different beliefs and histories within Japan?

A Seated Buddha

Which sects of Buddhism were especially valued in Japan? Why?

This sculpture of the Buddha suggests meditation. How were the Japanese garden and tea ceremony conducive to meditation? What other art forms shared in this mood of quiet, reflective austerity?

Photograph of the Golden Pavilion in Kyoto

Who were the shoguns? What "chores" made such peaceful retreats necessary?

Why is harmony one of the primary aesthetic values of Japanese art? What state is meant to be inspired in the viewer?

What Chinese influence do you see in the structure of the Golden Pavilion? What native Shinto elements are also present?

Ryoanji Temple Garden in Kyoto

Identify separately the following aesthetic elements in this garden: allusion, simplicity, restraint, and tranquility.

Has this garden, like the Golden Pavilion and the Seated Buddha above, been designed to promote a meditative state? Is this state merely sedentary? What elements of dynamism do you perceive?

Korean Art:

Vietnamese Art:

Photograph of the Temple of Literature, Hanoi

Why was the civil service examination so influential upon the governmental institutions and officials of China, Japan, Korea, and Vietnam?

How did this examination interact with the tradition of inherited nobility and office? Did the assertion of meritocracy supercede aristocracy in Vietnam?

Photograph of the One-Pillar Pagoda, Hanoi

What was sinification? How does this building reflect that process in Vietnam?

How is the Vietnamese valuing of nature expressed architecturally here? What about the Vietnamese valuing of sons over daughters? Did women have a different status in Vietnam than in Japan or Korea? How did this change over time?

VII. Identifying Important Concepts Behind the Conclusion

The Conclusion to this chapter recalls the following key ideas:

1. Influence of Chinese culture

2. Resistance to Chinese political power

3. Patterns of leadership and culture in Japan, Korea, and Vietnam

Review these general concepts before moving on to the next chapter.

Chapter Twelve:
The Making of Europe and the World of the Byzantine Empire, 500-1300

I. Outlining the Chapter

Transformation of the Roman World
- New Germanic Kingdoms
  - Kingdom of the Franks
- Role of the Christian Church
  - Organization of the Church
  - Monks and Their Missions
- Charlemagne and the World of the Carolingians
  - Charlemagne as Emperor
  - An Intellectual Renewal

World of Feudalism
- Invasions of the Ninth and Tenth Centuries
- Development of Feudalism
- Nobility of the Middle Ages
  - Way of the Warrior
  - Aristocratic Women

Growth of European Kingdoms
- England in the High Middle Ages
- Growth of the French Kingdom
- Lands of the Holy Roman Empire
- Slavic Peoples of Central and Eastern Europe
  - Development of Russia

World of the Peasants
- New Agriculture
- Manorial System
- Daily Life of the Peasantry

New World of Trade and Cities
- Revival of Trade
- Growth of Cities
  - Daily Life in the Medieval City
- Industry in Medieval Cities

Christianity and Medieval Civilization
- Papal Monarchy
  - Reform of the Papacy
  - Church Supreme
- New Religious Orders and New Spiritual Ideals
- Popular Religion in the High Middle Ages

Intellectual and Artistic World of the High Middle Ages
- Rise of Universities
- Development of Scholasticism
- Vernacular Literature

Romanesque Architecture: "A White Mantle of Churches"
Gothic Cathedral

Byzantine Empire and the Crusades
Reign of Justinian (527-565)
From Eastern Roman to Byzantine Empire
Life in Constantinople
New Heights and New Problems
Crusades

Conclusion

II. Terms and Persons To Know

Germanic peoples

Ostrogoths

Theodoric

Visigoths

Angles and Saxons

Frankish kingdom

Clovis

Merovingian dynasty

Arian sect

Germanic law

wergeld

compurgation and ordeal

Christian church

bishops

popes

Gregory I

Papal states

monasticism

Saint Benedict

abbots and abbesses

Pepin

Charlemagne

Carolingian Empire

counts

Emperor of the Romans (see also chapter introduction)

Carolingian Renaissance

scriptoria

Charles the Bald, Louis the German, and Lothair

Magyars

Vikings

feudalism

vassal

knights

fief

subinfeudation

feudal contract

nobility

castles

chivalry

tournaments

lady of the castle

Eleanor of Aquitaine

Norman conquest

Henry II

Thomas Becket

Magna Carta

parliament

Capetians

Philip II

Estates-General

Otto I

Hohenstaufen dynasty

slavic peoples

Cyril and Methodius

Orthodox Christianity

"the Rus"

Kiev

Alexander Nevsky

advances in farming

manorialism

serfs

demesne

peasant life

revival of trade

commercial capitalism

burg

charters of liberty

city life

guilds

Investiture Controversy

papal supremacy

Cistercian monasticism

Hildegard of Bingen

Franciscans

Dominicans

Inquisition

popular religion: sacraments, saints, Virgin Mary, relics, indulgences

universities

scholasticism

Thomas Aquinas

vernacular literature

Romanesque churches

Gothic cathedrals

Abbot Suger

Eastern Roman Empire

Justinian

Belisarius

Code of Law

Byzantine Empire

Constantinople

Hagia Sophia

Macedonian emperors

Seljuk Turks

Alexius I

crusades

1453

III. Mapwork

Map 12.1. The New Kingdoms of the Old Western Empire

Identify the following on the map: Ostrogoths, Visigoths, Vandals, Byzantines, Angles, Saxons, and Franks. How did these kingdoms interact during the early middle ages? Which are Germanic? What city was the capital of the Byzantine empire?

How were the Franks able to unite? What role did Clovis' religion play in this achievement?

Map 12.2. The Carolingian Empire

Who bequeathed the Frankish kingdom to Charlemagne? By how much did Charlemagne increase this patrimony?

Consider this map in light of the primary source above, "The Achievements of Charlemagne." What is the importance of Aachen? Mainz? Rome? The Byzantines? Does Einhard accurately describe (in the first paragraph of that passage) the geographical regions conquered by his king?

Map 12.3. Europe in the High Middle Ages

What role did the Papal States play in medieval politics?

How does this map presage the formation of the modern states of Eastern and Western Europe?

What were the pressures on the Byzantine Empire?

How do the Crusades reflect political and religious differences between Western Europe and the Middle East? Between Christianity and Islam?

Map 12.4. The World of the Slavs

When did Asian nomads begin to move into Eastern Europe? What effect did their movements have on local populations? What ultimate effect did their migrations have on their own identity?

Why is a distinction made between western, southern, and eastern Slavs? What especially distinguishes the western Slavs from the other two groups?

Who founded Kiev? Who introduced Orthodoxy to this region? What role did the Mongols play in the history of "the Rus"?

Map 12.5. A Manor

What is manorialism? What technological advances in farming bettered this system during the middle ages?

Why was land of primary importance to feudalism? How did serfs fit into this political structure? How did their role, and the role of their lords, change over time?

Briefly describe rural versus town life in the middle ages. What advantages did the *burg* offer a peasant who left his lord's demesne? On the other hand, what advantages did seasonal rural existence have over town life?

Map 12.6. The Byzantine Empire in the Time of Justinian

What lasting effect was the Byzantine empire to have on Russian culture?

What are the differences between Roman and Eastern Orthodox forms of Catholicism? Where on this map would the line be drawn between the two?

How did the Fourth Crusade affect the Byzantine empire? Why did Alexius I call to the West for help?

Why were Justinian's successors unable to hold the vast territories Belisarius had gained?

What role did the Seljuk and Ottoman Turks play in the history of Constantinople?

Map 12.7. The Early Crusades

Which European kings played leading roles in the crusades? Which popes?

Why do some scholars believe that the crusades had a beneficial effect on European society, even though they ultimately failed?

What happened to the children who embarked on the final crusade?

IV. Datework

Chapter Timeline: From the Rise of the Germanic Kingdoms to the Emergence of English Parliament

What peoples comprised the Germanic kingdoms? How did each respond to the legacy of the Roman Empire?

Why is the reign of Charlemagne referred to as a Carolingian renaissance? How many years lapsed between the deposition of the last Roman emperor and the crowning of Charlemagne as Emperor of the Romans?

Why did church and state engage in the investiture controversy? Which king opposed Gregory VII on the investiture issue? How was this resolved?

How did King John's signing of the Magna Carta lead to the eventual formation of the English Parliament?

How many crusades were there? Why did they fail? Did they all have the same purpose?

Chronology: The European Kingdoms

What lasting effects did the Norman Conquest have on English history?

What lasting effects did the Magna Carta have on the English monarchy?

What conflicts led to the development of the First parliament in England and the Estates-General in France? How were Edward I and Philip IV responsible?

Why was the "holy empire" of Frederick I and II of Germany problematic? What role does the pope play in its downfall?

Why do Russians consider Alexander Nevsky a great hero in Russian history?

Chronology: The Crusades

Were the crusades justified? Who called for these expeditions?

Which of the crusades were successful? Which failed? Ultimately, what was their effect on Western Europe? On the Byzantine empire? On the Middle East?

Why did the crusading spirit become linked to the persecution of European Jews?

V. Primary Sourcework

Medieval European Primary Sources:

Germanic Customary Law: The Ordeal

What has been proved by the ordeal Gregory of Tours describes? How?

Why do the Arian presbyter and the Catholic deacon each call one another "heretic"?

What other provisions of Germanic law provided for remedies on a very personal basis? How was this different from previous Roman law?

The Achievements of Charlemagne: Einhard, *Life of Charlemagne*

Since Einhard arrived at the Carolingian court in 791 or 792, how long could he have known Charlemagne? Does this excerpt reflect close, personal knowledge of Charlemagne, his court, and his works?

According to Einhard, what was Charlemagne's relation with the church?

Who were the "wild and barbarous" tribes Charlemagne subdued?

Was Charlemagne actually Emperor of the Romans? How did he get this title? Is Einhard correct about the reaction of the Emperors of Constantinople to Charlemagne's assumption of that title?

Murder in the Cathedral: John of Salisbury to John of Canterbury, Bishop of Poitiers

Why did Henry II cry out, "Who will free me of this priest"? What was the ultimate result of his outburst for his own stance on clerical crimes and the church courts?

How do Becket's last words reflect the elements of medieval popular religion?

Why did these knights' specific status as vassals of Henry II result in their murder of an archbishop?

A Muslim's Description of the Rus: Ibn Fadlan, *Description of the Rus*

What evidence does Ibn Fadlan provide for the Viking origin of medieval Russian culture?

Why did this Muslim author find the Rus "the filthiest of God's creatures"? What is his judgement on the sexual behavior he observes?

According to Ibn Fadlan, how do the Rus treat their slaves? the sick? Serfs? Criminals? Do you find his account credible?

The Medieval City: The King's Command to Boutham

The king is very concerned about pigsties in this document. What other practices contributed to pollution in medieval cities?

Is the king more concerned for the health of Boutham's citizens, or for his ministers?

Why would the king's ministers visit the city? How did medieval towns generally govern themselves? What exceptional privileges were granted to the cities by their territorial lords?

A Miracle of Saint Bernard

What were the ideological differences between the Cistercian, Franciscan, and Dominican orders?

What is the original root of the word "monk"? How has the monk described here become a renegade?

What two miracles occur in this excerpt from the life of St. Bernard? How does this text about a saint reflect popular religious practices during the middle ages?

A Western View of the Byzantine Empire: Liudprand of Cremona, *Antapodosis*

What evidence do you detect in this passage of Liudprand's mixed feelings about Byzantium?

Do you suppose that Constantine VII was impressed by Liudprand's gifts from Berengar? Why or why not?

How does the appearance of Constantine VII in this excerpt reflect the Byzantine emperor's role in society? How was this role different from that of emperors in the west?

Treatment of the Jews: The Jews and the Ritual Murder of Christian Children and
The Regulations of Avignon, 1243

Why were Muslims and Jews seen as enemies of Christianity in the middle ages?

On the basis of what evidence did the people of Gloucester decide that Jews had killed an eight-year-old boy? What Jewish rituals are mentioned here? Does the author understand them?

VI. Artwork

Medieval European Art:

The Baptism of Clovis

What is Arianism? Why was it politically advantageous for Clovis to be baptized a Catholic Christian?

How does the Arian-Catholic conflict within the church foreshadow the later medieval concern with heresies? The rise of the Inquisition?

What factors would later enable Pepin to depose the Merovingian dynasty Clovis founded?

In this manuscript illumination, what statement is the artist making about the relative importance of church and secular (even kingly) power? Who was the artist in all probability? Has this affected the depiction of Clovis and the bishops?

Why are the nobles all clustered to one side, and the bishops to the other? What symbols of office does each side offer the Merovingian king?

The Coronation of Charlemagne

Did Pope Leo III and Charlemagne plan his coronation openly? Was Charlemagne aware of the pope's plan to crown him emperor? Why is this question subject to an ambiguous answer?

By what authority did the Bishop of Rome claim the title of *papa*, or pope? How did this claim divide Western Catholicism from Eastern Orthodoxy?

Why did this coronation benefit both the pope and Charlemagne?

The Vikings Attack England

From where did the Vikings originate? Where do they finally settle down? How are they absorbed into European civilization?

What technological features of Viking ships enabled them to be successful raiders?

The Tournament

What purposes, other than entertainment, did melées and tournaments serve? Were they considered serious preparation for warfare?

How did a man become a knight? What code of values ideally accompanied his warrior abilities?

Why are there no women on the field? What important roles were open to them within the medieval nobility?

Peasants in the Manorial System

What is the difference between a serf and a slave?

Where would the bailiff fit within feudal society? Who would have been his employer?

What products, in addition to grain, were significant in European markets? What factors allowed trade to revive and flourish during the middle ages in Europe?

Briefly describe the two-field and the three-field system of cultivation. What did the latter make possible? How did the new plow help?

Shops in a Medieval Town

What was a guild? What distinguised an apprentice, a journeyman, and a master?

In what sense were the earliest universities guilds?

Who were burghers? Were they part of the feudal system?

Consider this work alongside the primary souce immediately following, "The Medieval City." Despite the luxury, beauty and industry portrayed in this illustration, what unpleasant environmental facts characterized medieval towns?

A Group of Nuns

Were abbesses as authoritative and influential as abbots in the middle ages?

Who was Hildegard of Bingen, and what was her contribution to the medieval church?

Why might the monastery be an attractive way of life for women in this era? What alternatives were available to them?

A University Classroom

What was the meaning of the Latin word *universitas*? How does understanding this word contribute to our understanding of the first universities in Europe?

What were the first two universities in Europe?

Why were classes called "lectures"? What courses comprised a medieval curriculum? Why did individual courses contain no tests?

Explain the degrees available to students at medieval universities. Which professions were most valued? Are these standards and values relevant today?

Two photographs: Barrel Vaulting and
The Gothic Cathedral

Consider these two photographs in sequence. How did Romanesque architecture differ from the Gothic style? What technological advances made Gothic cathedrals possible?

What values are reflected in the explosion of church building in the middle ages?

Byzantine Art:

The Emperor Justinian Surrounded by His Court

How is the Eastern Roman emperor depicted here in both his civic and religious role? How is the military included?

Why is Justinian remembered for his contribution to Roman law? To the law of Europe?

What were the achievements of Justinian's general Belisarius? Of the Macedonian rulers of the Byzantine empire? What external pressures cause the decline of this culture?

In the earlier primary source reading "The Achievements of Charlemagne," Einhard noted that Charlemagne had to import columns from Rome and Ravenna for his building projects. What does such a statement indicate about the relative wealth and power of the Byzantine and Carolingian empires?

Interior View of Hagia Sophia

Why are Koranic inscriptions now decorating what was built to be an Orthodox church? What historical event is reflected in this transformation?

With what other architectural monuments did Justinian adorn Constantinople? Why is this city sometimes called "the second Rome"?

How does Hagia Sophia differ from the Romanesque and Gothic churches pictured earlier in this chapter?

VII. Identifying Important Concepts Behind the Conclusion

The Conclusion to this chapter recalls the following key ideas:

1. political institutions from the Germanic states and the Carolingian empire to the kings of the new European civilization

2. German tribes, Roman legacy, and Christian church

3. intellectual, spiritual and institutional revivals, including the papacy, feudalism, scholasticism, and the rise of European cities and universities

4. Byzantine empire from Justinian to the fall of the empire in 1453

Review these general concepts before moving on to the next chapter.

Chapter Thirteen
Crisis and Rebirth: Europe in the Fourteenth and Fifteenth Centuries

I. Outlining the Chapter

A Time of Troubles: Black Death and Social Crisis
- Famine and Black Death
- Economic Disclocation and Social Upheaval
  - Family Life and Gender Roles in Late Medieval Cities
- Economic Recovery

Political Instability and Political Renewal
- Hundred Years' War
- Political Instability
- Political Recovery: The "New Monarchies"
  - Western Europe
  - Central Europe: The Holy Roman Empire
  - Eastern Europe
- Ottoman Turks and the End of the Byzantine Empire
- Italian States
- Machiavelli and the New Statecraft

Decline of the Church
- Boniface VIII and the Conflict with the State
- Papacy at Avignon (1305-1378)
- Great Schism
- Problems of Heresy and Reform
- Renaissance Papacy

Meaning and Characteristics of the Italian Renaissance

Social Changes in the Renaissance
- Social Classes: The Nobility
- Social Classes: The Third Estate of Peasants and Townspeople
- Family and Marriage in Renaissance Italy

Intellectual Renaissance in Italy
- Italian Renaissance Humanism
  - Humanism and Philosophy
- Education in the Renaissance
- Development of Vernacular Literature
- Impact of Printing

Artistic Renaissance

- Northern Artistic Renaissance

Conclusion

II. Terms and Persons To Know

famine

Black Death

Yersinia pestis

flagellants

anti-Semitism

Statute of Laborers

Jacquerie

English Peasants' Revolt of 1381

Wat Tyler and John Ball

Richard II

ciompi

family life

gender roles

Hansa or Hanseatic League

industry

Medici family

duchy of Gascony

Hundred Years' War

Edward III

Henry V

Joan of Arc

political instability

"new monarchies"

Louis XI

Henry VII

Isabella of Castile and Ferdinand of Aragon

hermandades

Inquisition

Jews and Muslims

Habsburg dynasty

Eastern Europe

Sejm

Corvinus

Ivan III

Ottoman Turks

Paleologus dynasty

Constantinople

Italian States: Milan, Venice, and Florence

Visconti and Sforza rulers

condotticre

Cosimo de' Medici

Federigo da Montefeltro

Isabella d'Este

sack of Rome

Niccolò Machiavelli

The Prince

"fullness of power"

Boniface III

Unam Sanctam

Philip IV

Clement V

Avignon

Great Schism

conciliarism

Councils of Pisa and Constance

John Hus

Renaissance papacy

Julius II

nepotism

Alexander VI

Saint Peter's Basilica

Leo X

Renaissance

urban society

Greco-Roman culture

individualism

humanism

l'uomo universale

the three estates

Baldassare Castiglione

The Book of the Courtier

peasants and townspeople

marriage

humanism

Petrarch

Leonardo Bruni

New Cicero

revival of Greek literature

Marsilio Ficino

Neoplatonism

Hermeticism

magi

Pico della Mirandola

Oration on the Dignity of Man

humanist schools

liberal studies

Dante

Divine Comedy

Geoffrey Chaucer

The Canterbury Tales

printing press

Gutenburg Bible

naturalism

Masaccio

perspective

anatomy

Leonardo da Vinci

Raphael

Michelangelo

Jan van Eyck

Albrecht Dürer

III. Mapwork

Map 13.1. Spread of the Black Death

By what other names is the Black Death known? Why?

Where did this disease originate? What factors caused it to affect Europe so severely in the fourteenth century?

How did the "little ice age" contribute to the devastation of the Black Death?

Why were the southern, or Mediterranean regions of Western Europe affected first? Which regions were affected last? Why?

Map 13.2. Europe in the Fifteenth Century

What changes in the monarchy occurred in the fifteenth century in France, England, and Spain?

Which monarchs and their policies effected these changes?

How did the Holy Roman Empire and Eastern Europe fare differently? Why?

Map 13.3. The Italian States in the Fifteenth Century

Why do some historians view the Milan, Venice, and Florence as the first true examples of the modern secular state?

Why are the printing press with moveable type, the rise of libraries and schools of art, and the revival of classical building styles all important for understanding the term *Renaissance* in Italy?

Which independent city-states on this map were also of primary importance in fifteenth-century politics, trade, and culture?

What aspects of the pope's administration of the Papal States led to criticism of that religious office?

IV. Datework

Chapter Timeline: From the Hundred Years' War to the High Renaissance

How long were there popes in residence at Avignon? Why? How was this conflict resolved?

For how long did the Black Death devastate Europe? Is this whole time period reflected in this chapter?

How did the Hundred Years' war lead to peasant revolts in France and in England? How did these revolts differ?

How do the writers and artists of the Renaissance reflect the value placed in this period upon the concept of *l'uomo universale*?

Chronology: The Hundred Years' War

Why did the duchy of Gascony play such a leading role in the outbreak of the Hundred Years' War?

What impact did the traditional medieval values of knighthood and vassalage have upon the war's inception and progress?

What was the ultimate result for the English throne? For the French monarchy? For French peasants?

Was the battle of Agincourt decisive? How did Joan of Arc save the French throne for Charles?

Chronology: the European States

Why was Louis XI called "the Spider"? Why are his policies today considered to have built the basis for the strong French monarchy of later years?

What great successes in government were achieved by Henry VII, the first Tudor king?

What were the policies of Ferdinand and Isabella of Spain in regard to Muslims and Jews? How was this related to their sponsorship of the Inquisiton?

Briefly describe the rise of the Habsburg dynasty following the failure of the Hohenstaufens.

What was the relation between Russia and the Mongols? Why is Ivan III remembered as a great prince of Moscow?

Chronology: The Italian States

What did the patronage of Cosimo de Medici contribute to Italian Renaissance humanism?

Who were the Visconti? The Sforzas? The Medici? What relation did these families have with the Italian papacy? With *condottieri*?

Why do the English king Charles VIII and the Spanich king Charles I invade Italy and sack Rome?

Chronology: The Decline of the Church

Why did Pope Boniface VIII and the French king Philip IV come into conflict?

How does this conflict reflect the larger issue of papal vs. secular (or spiritual vs. temporal) power in Europe?

At its worst, how many popes at one time claimed leadership of the Catholic Church during the Great Schism? Under what authority did each make his claim?

Why does the Great schism lead to conciliarism? What do the Councils of Pisa and of Constance hope to achieve? Are they successful?

What political and cultural activities are important to the Renaissance popes? Why are such activities open to criticism, such as those voiced by John Hus?

V. Primary Sourcework

Fourteenth-Century Primary Sources:

A Medieval Holocaust: The Cremation of the Stasbourg Jews

What is the name of the bacterium that causes the "greatest epidemic" described by the author? What do the people of Strasbourg believe is causing this disease?

Why did the anti-Semitism of towns such as Strasbourg lead to the establishment of large Jewish populations in Eastern Europe?

Why were those Jews "who wanted to baptize themselves" spared?

Why does the author state that "The money was indeed the thing that killed the Jews"?

A Revolt of French Peasants: Jean Froissart, *Chronicles*

What features of this passage indicate that it is an excerpt from the chronicle of a French aristocrat?

To what historical events does Froissart refer when he mentions that the peasants' acts were "worse than anything that ever took place between Christians and Saracens [Turks, or more generally, Muslims]"? Why would he use those events as a standard for barbarous crimes?

Why does the author emphasize the peasants' cruelty to women and children?

What enabled the peasants' initial success in the *Jacquerie*?

Fifteenth-Century Primary Source:

The Trial of Joan of Arc

Why was Joan of Arc feared by the English and the Burgundians? What role had Burgundy played in the Hundred Years' War?

What did Joan's voice tell her? According to fifteenth-century belief, what were the possible sources of visions? Why was her testimony considered to demonstrate heresy?

What effect did she have on the Battle of Orleans?

Sixteenth-Century Primary Source:

The Letters of Isabella d'Este

What do these letters demonstrate about Isabella's character? About her political acumen?

Why did Francesco Gonzaga respond so violently to her refusal? What might have happened to her son had she turned him over as hostage? What might have happened to her husband the duke if she did not?

How did Isabella try to resolve this conflict of loyalties? Who governed Mantua after her husband's death?

Fourteenth-Century Primary Source:

Boniface VIII's Defense of Papal Supremacy: Pope Boniface VIII, *Unam Sanctam*

What special relationship with God does Boniface VIII claim in this excerpt?

Why did the pope issue this bull? What effect did he hope this document would have upon temporal rulers?

How did the fate of Pope Boniface VIII lead to the Great Schism?

Why was the Great Schism so detrimental to the reputation of the Papacy? To the Catholic Church as a whole?

Fifteenth-Century Primary Sources:

Marriage Negotiations: Alessandra Strozzi to Her Son Filippo in Naples

Why did the Florentine matron Alessandra Strozzi not approach Francesco Tanagli herself?

What considerations are paramount for a "fine marriage"? Why?

What evidence does this document provide for the responsibilities and education expected for young Italian noblewomen in the fifteenth century?

Pico della Mirandola and the *Oration on the Dignity of Man*

How was Pico della Mirandola influeced by Neoplatonism and by Hermeticism? What evidence do you see for these Renaissance philosophies here?

How does this document, by giving Adam a speech not found in the Old Testament, depart from medieval standards of piety? What Renaissance ideals does the author consider more important?

Fourteenth-Century Primary Source:

Dante's Vision of Hell: Dante, "Inferno," from *The Divine Comedy*

What are the three major divisions of Dante's *Divine Comedy*? Who serves as his guide in these regions?

Why did Dante people his literary vision of hell with so many Florentines?

How are Dante and Chaucer together important for understanding the rise of vernacular literature? Which language is being left behind? Which languages do these works promote?

VI. Artwork

Late Medieval and Renaissance Art:

Mass Burial of Plague Victims

Consider this artwork in combination with Map 13.1. What might have caused certain isolated regions to escape from the plague relatively unharmed?

Elsewhere in Europe, what were the consequences of this disease? How high do some scholars estimate that the death toll rose?

What effect did the disease have on the lives of those who lived?

Who were the flagellants, and why did the Catholic church eradicate this movement?

Peasant Rebellion

Why is the *Jacquerie* considered a "revolt of desperation," while the English Peasants' Revolt of 1381 is considered a revolt of "rising expectations"?

Which of the three "estates" were involved in these revolts? How were the French and English peasants' aims similar?

Who prevailed in these conflicts? How?

Harbor Scene at Hamburg

How did the economic depression of the fourteenth century affect fifteenth-century patterns of manufacturing in Europe?

What significant changes occurred in industry and banking during the fifteenth century?

What was the role of the Hanseatic League?

Who received the monies collected by customs officials? To what uses was such income put?

Joan of Arc

Why was Joan of Arc killed? What were the roles of Henry V, Charles, and the Inquisition in her life story?

How does this miniature portrait reflect what she called herself, "the Maid"?

Why was she later made a saint?

Piero della Francesca, *Duke and Duchess of Urbino*

In what ways did Urbino represent a typical high Renaissance cultural center?

Do you think that Machiavelli would have admired Federigo de Montefeltro? Why or why not?

What roles were open to aristocratic women of the Italian Renaissance city-states? How does Isabella d'Este represent these possibilities?

How is the rebirth of the art of perspective demonstrated in these portraits?

A Renaissance Pope: Sixtus IV

How did Sixtus IV, along with Alexander VI, Julius II, and Leo X, conceive of the duties of the pope? How did each pursue and discharge his office?

Why is papal patronage essential to the revival of Greco-Roman learning in Italy?

What Greek and Latin works of literature were most important to aristocratic and papal Renaissance libraries? Why?

Wedding Banquet

How has the newly revived technique of perspective in painting been employed by Botticelli in this painting? Has concern with anatomy and movement been equally important to the artist?

How has the artist depicted the wealth of the two families? Who is likely to have commissioned the painting? For what purpose?

Early Renaissance Painting:

Masaccio, *Tribute Money*

What evidence does this painting provide for Masaccio's innovations with realism? With perspective?

How does his subject matter link Masaccio to the medieval tradition?

High Renaissance Paintings:

Leonardo da Vinci, *The Last Supper*

What evidence does this painting provide for the High Renaissance concern for idealism? How does this differ from Masaccio's concern with realism?

How has Leonardo carefully depicted each person's character and inner nature in this painting?

Is the finished product a series of thirteen portraits, or a coherent painting? How has Leonardo achieved this result?

Raphael, *The Alba Madonna*

Distinguish in this painting the presence of balance, harmony, clarity, and rational composition. How are these artistic goals Neoplatonic in origin?

How did Italian Renaissance painting differ in style from Northern Renaissance painting? How did Michelangelo summarize the differences?

How is Renaissance humanism reflected in this painting?

Michelangelo, *Creation of Adam*

What similarities do you perceive between the ideals reflected in this painting and the ideals expressed by Pico della Mirandola in his *Oration on the Dignity of Man* (presented earlier in the chapter)? What relation between man and God is expressed in both?

What relationship existed between the popes of the Italian Renaissance and Masacio, Leonardo da Vinci, Raphael, and Michelangelo?

Might the "spark" Adam waits to receive be the gift of individualism and freedom? What Renaissance institutions and ideals might suggest this?

How do Neoplatonic principles inform this work?

Northern Renaissance Paintings:

Jan van Eyck, *Giovanni Arnolfini and His Bride*

Why was the city of Bruges significant to European trade during the fourteenth and early fifteenth centuries? How is that importance reflected in this painting?

Identify the Northern concern for masterful detail and realistic portraiture in this painting. How has van Eyck skilfully used the illusion of daylight to illuminate both techniques?

Albrecht Dürer, *Adoration of the Magi*

What "Northern" and "Italian" influences do you perceive in this altarpiece?

How are both techniques reflective of the artist's life and training?

VII. Identifying Important Concepts Behind the Conclusion

The Conclusion to this chapter recalls the following key ideas:

1. Disintegration and rebirth in European societies during the fourteenth and fifteenth centuries

2. Political and religious conflicts of the Renaissance

3. Renaissance intellectuals and artists: art, philosophy, humanism, and the liberal education

Review these general concepts, and read the following section titled "Reflection: New Patterns of Civilization," before moving on to the next chapter.

Chapter Fourteen
New Encounters: The Creation of a World Market

I. Outlining the Chapter

Age of Exploration and Expansion
- Islam and the Spice Trade
- A New Player Enters the Game
- Development of a Portuguese Maritime Empire
- Voyages to the "New World"
  - Administration of the Spanish Empire in the New World
- Impact of European Expansion
- New Rivals Enter the Scene

Africa in an Era of Transition
- Slave Trade
- Political and Social Structures in a Changing Continent

Southeast Asia in the Era of the Spice Trade
- Building Stable Political Systems on the Mainland
- Arrival of the West
  - Government and Politics
  - Economy
  - Daily Life

Conclusion

II. Terms and Persons To Know

Vasco da Gama

Malacca

spice trade

Marco Polo

Renaissance European expansion

economic motive

religious zeal

portolani

navigational techniques

Prince Henry the Navigator

Calicut

Admiral Alfonso de Albuquerque

monopoly

Christopher Columbus

Queen Isabella of Spain

"America"

"New World"

Treaty of Tordesillas

conquistadors

Hernan Cortés

Francisco Pizarro

"Indios"

encomienda

European diseases

Spanish administrative system

viceroys

gold and silver

New agricultural products

Ferdinand Magellan

Sir Francis Drake

English East India Company

Dutch East India Company or VOC

Dutch West India Company

Francisco de Almeida

Mwene Metapa

Mozambique

Bantu peoples

Tutsi pastoralists

Cape of Good Hope

Boers

kingdom of Songhai

Askia Mohammad

slave trade

sugar

mortality rates

dislocating effects

Morocco

Ashanti kingdom

Swahili culture

Benin

"golden stool"

Ibo

European influence

Islam in Africa

Wahhabism

Christianity in sub-Saharan Afirca

Philippine Islands

Spice Islands

factories

Thai peoples

Vietnamese

Dutch-Portuguese spice conflicts

French-English spice conflicts

trade and missionary privileges

intervention in local politics

mainland states

Malay states

Buddhist style of kingship

karma

Javanese style of kingship

wahyu

priyayi

Muslim influence

sultan

Muslim-animist conflict

agriculture

commerce

regional and interregional trade

daily life

religious beliefs

batik

wayang kulit

III. Mapwork

Map 14.1. European Possessions in the West Indies

Why were the regions depicted here originally known as "the West Indies"? How were they discovered by Europeans?

How did America get its name? How did the "Indians"?

What was the significance of the Treaty of Tordesillas for the European powers interested in the New World?

Which countries had the largest settlements? Why?

Map 14.2. European Voyages and Possessions in the Sixteenth and Seventeenth Centuries

What new products entered European markets, and European agriculture, as a result of the voyages of exploration depicted here?

Why did the Portuguese ultimately lose their advantageous position as preeminent explorers, sea traders, and empire builders? What voyages had won this for them in the first place?

Locate Malacca on the map. Why is this site so important for the history of the European-Asian spice trade?

Map 14.3. The Slave Trade

What type of labor were African slaves destined for in the New World? Why were Native Americans not considered a sufficient labor force?

How did slavery in the Americas differ from older types of slavery in Africa? In the Middle East? In Europe?

How did slave traders acquire African slaves? How many were shipped across the Atlantic before such trade was outlawed?

Why did the Dutch settle at the Cape of Good Hope? Who were the *Boers*?

Map 14.4. The Pattern of World Trade

Note the location of spice ports on the map. What particular spices were especially prized on the European market? Why? What class distinctions are reflected in this trade?

How many of the goods listed here are necessities? How many are luxuries? What do your answers indicate about the world trade system sketched here?

IV. Datework

Chapter Timeline: From the Voyages of Columbus to the Americas to the Expulsion of the Portuguese from Mombasa

How many European nations explored the Americas during the fifteenth and sixteenth centuries?

What motivated explorers? Conquistadors? Traders? Were their motives similar, or racially different?

Why were slaves brought to the New World? Why had they been used in Africa? In the Old World?

What is the significance of the term "New World"? Why did explorers from the "Old World" use it? Where is the "Old World"? What made it seem older?

Chronology: Spanish Activities in the Americas

Why did Christopher Columbus sail west, not east, in search of the Indies? How many voyages did he make?

Why do scholars distinguish between Columbus' voyages and Cortés' and Pizarro's conquests?

What governmental structure was created in South America in order to carry out Spanish rule? What role did the viceroys play?

Chronology: The Penetration of Africa

Describe the Portuguese achievements in world exploration and trade between the life of Prince Henry the Navigator and the Portuguese expulsion from Mombasa. Were the Portuguese more successful in the east or in the west? Why?

Why was Christianity so much less successful than Islam in sub-Saharan Africa?

Describe foreign influences upon the Ashanti kingdom in Western Africa, and the Swahili kingdom in East Africa.

Chronology: The Spice Trade

Who is famous for the phrase "Gold and Christians"? What is meant by this? In what way does this brief statement capture the essence of Western interests in Southeast Asia in the sixteenth century and seventeenth centuries?

Briefly describe the differences between the English East India Company, the Dutch East India Company, and the Dutch West India Company. Why were these ventures formed? Who invested in them?

Where were the Dutch and Portuguese competing for trade in the East? For what products? Which sites are most important in these conflicts?

How did the French and English vie for missionary privileges in Southeast Asia?

V. Primary Sourcework

Primary Sources on World Exploration and Trade:

The Portuguese Conquest of Malacca: *The Commentaries of the Great Alfonso de Albuquerque, Second Viceroy of India*

Why did the Portuguese attack Malacca? What was the result?

Was Albuquerque primarily concerned with trade issues, or with missionary goals?

To whom does Albuquerque address himself here? Why does he make the arguments he does concerning Cairo, Mecca and Venice?

Las Casas and the Spanish Treatment of the American Natives: Bartolomé de Las Casas, *The Tears of the Indians*

What evidence do you see here for the *encomienda* system? What was the intention of this administrative policy? How did Queen Isabella's plans for the *encomienda* system lead to abuse?

What evidence do you perceive in this passage that lends credence to some scholars' opinion that Las Casas may have exaggerated his account?

An Aztec's Lament: *Flowers and Songs of Sorrow*

Why has the author of this poetic memoir decided that his creator is "weary" and "angry"?

King of Songhai: *The Epic of Askia Mohammed*

For what two reasons did Askia Mohammed travel to Mecca?

How did the traditional *kafu* system lead to the decline of his kingdom?

When did the English, French, and Dutch become active in West Africa? Is this related to the fall of Songhai?

Why was Mamar Kssaye revered by his people? How did he consolidate his power?

A Slave Market in Africa: A Firsthand Report

Consider this passage in light of Map 14.3, which depicts the slave trade. Why did the slave trade increase so dramatically in Africa after the arrival of Europeans in the New World?

Why does the Dutch author state that this trade "must go on"?

Why does this Dutch observer find Dutch practices in slaving superior to those of the French, Portuguese, and English?

The Great City of Timbuktu: Leo Africanus, *History and Description of Africa*

What are the most valuable trade commodities mentioned by Leo Africanus? How did these goods figure in the Morroco-Songhai conflicts of the sixteenth century?

By "Barbary," the author refers to Arabia. What Arabian influences are important in this excerpt? How have they come to Timbuktu?

What evidence does this document provide for the importance of Timbuktu as a center of learning?

Christianity in the Congo: Duarte Lopez at the Court of the King of the Congo

According to Lopez, how did the possession of Portuguese goods come to distinguish the social classes in the Congo? Which items were especially prized?

Why has the king's conversion resulted in "imitation of...the king of Portugal"?

Why did this Portuguese author travel to the Congo? Has his role there influenced this account?

An Exchange of Royal Correspondence: A Letter to the King of Tonkin from Louis XIV

Why might Louis XIV have been unaware of already extant missionary activity in Vietnam?

Why does the king of France wish to establish the "Royal Company" in Vietnam "as soon as possible"?

What "ancient custom" would the head of the Trinh family have meant when he mentioned that one forbade the introduction of Christianity?

The Timely End of Sultan Zainal-'Abidin: *The History of Acheh*

Locate Acheh on Map 14.4. Why was this site important in the world spice trade system?

Why would the strategic and commercial significance of Acheh have contributed to its early conversion to Islam?

What similarities do you perceive between the habits of Sultan Zainal-'Abidin and the Roman gladitorial combats and games described in Chapter Four?

VI. Artwork

The Art of Exploration:

A Sixteenth-Century Map of Africa

Who was Prester John? Why did Europeans with missionary tendencies desire to discover his kingdom?

What advances in map-making occurred in fifteenth-century Euope? What were the *portolani*?

Which navigational techniques aided European explorers? Why were certain wind patterns known as "trade winds"?

What African sites has the mapmaker considered important? What evidence do you see here that sea trade was not the only method for trading with Africans?

Photograph of Sailboat near Zanzibar

Which products were prevalent in East African trade? In West Africa?

When did the Portuguese establish a presence in East Africa?

Why was not merely commerce, but a monopoly desired by both Muslims and Europeans?

The Caravel, Workhorse of the Age of Exploration

Compare this period engraving with the preceding photograph of a boat near Zanzibar. What is a lateen sail? What advantages and disadvantages does this sailing technology involve?

Why did the design of the *Santa Maria* combine both Mediterranean and European ship styles?

Columbus Lands in the New World

Was Columbus an explorer or a conquistador? What was the difference?

What European beliefs and attitudes about "New World" people are reflected here?

From where would the artist have learned the information necessary to create such a painting?

Photograph of the Seat of Argentine Independence

For how many years did the Spanish control Argentina? Which other South American countries were under Spanish rule?

What influences are still visible in South America today as a result of the Spanish presence? Where were the Portuguese more important?

Photograph of the Strait of Magellan

Why was Ferdinand Magellan seeking a western route to the Spice Islands?

What lasting result did his voyage have on the Philippines?

What toll did Magellan's voyage take on his fleet? On his men?

A Slave Ship

Why would a drawing like this one have been produced and published?

Where are the men? The women? How much room is provided for boys? For girls? Why are children present? Were children always a part of the slave trade? Why are there more men than women depicted?

Why did the production of the crop sugar specifically lead to such inhumane practices?

Photograph of the Great Gate at Marrakech

What effect did Morocco have on the kingdom of Songhai?

Which commodities were especially important in this trade dispute?

Photograph of the Thai Capital at Ayuthaya

Why are the Thai remembered as a warlike people from medieval times onward in Southeast Asia?

Briefly describe the Buddhist and Javanese styles of kingship in Southeast Asia. How is the Buddhist faith reflected in these architectural monuments?

Photograph of Ship Bringing Lumber to Java

What similarities do you perceive between this pinisi and the caravel in the first photograph in this chapter? Why would such similarities exist?

Consider this photograph alongside Map 14.4. Where was timber most important in the world trade system depicted there?

Your Ancestors Are Watching You!

Although the burial customs depicted here are unique, what other Asian and Southeast Asian countries stressed ancestral rites and the continuing presence of the ancestors in the lives of the living community?

VII. Identifying Important Concepts Behind the Conclusion

The Conclusion to this chapter recalls the following key ideas:

1. European exploration and domination of world trade

2. Consequent changes in America, Africa, South Asia, and Southeast Asia

Review these general concepts, and review the section preceding this chapter, "The Emergence of New World Patterns, 1500-1800," before moving on to the next chapter.

Chapter Fifteen: Religious Reform and State Building in Europe

I. Outlining the Chapter

Protestant Reformation
- Prelude to Reformation
- Church and Religion on the Eve of the Reformation
- Martin Luther and the Reformation in Germany
- Spread of the Protestant Reformation
- Social Impact of the Protestant Reformation
  - Family
  - Religious Practices and Popular Culture

Catholic Reformation

Europe in Crisis: War, Revolution, and Social Disintegration, 1560-1650
- Politics and the Wars of Religion in the Sixteenth Century
  - French Wars of Religion (1562-1598)
  - Philip II and the Cause of Militant Catholicism
  - The England of Elizabeth
- Economic and Social Crises: The Witchcraft Craze
- Seventeenth-Century Crises: Revolution and War
  - Thirty Years' War (1618-1648)

Response to Crisis: The Practice of Absolutism
- Practice of Absolutism: France under Louis XIV
- Absolutism in Central and Eastern Europe
  - From Muscovy to Russia

Limited Monarchy: England and the Emergence of Constitutional Monarchy
- Revolution and Civil War
- Restoration and a Glorious Revolution
- Responses to Revolution

World of European Culture
- Art
- Golden Age of Literature: England and Spain
- Theatre: The Triumph of French Neoclassicism

Conclusion

II. Terms and Persons To Know

Protestant Reformation

Martin Luther

Christian humanists

Erasmus

philosophy of Christ

Renaissance popes

finances

relics

Modern Devotion

The Imitation of Christ

justification by faith

Bible as sole authority

Ninety-five Theses

indulgences

Pope Leo X

Charles V

Edict of Worms

Peasants' War

Peace of Augsburg

Zwinglianism

Ulrich Zwingli

Calvinism

John Calvin

predestination

Geneva

English Reformation

Henry VIII

Thomas Cranmer

Book of Common Prayer

Queen Mary

Anabaptists

celibacy

role of women

popular religious practices

Catholic Reformation or Counter-Reformation

Jesuits

Ignatius of Loyola

reformed papacy

Pope Paul III

Pope Paul IV

Council of Trent

French Wars of Religion

Huguenots

ultra-Catholics

Henry IV

Edict of Nantes

Philip II

Netherlands

William of Nassau

Peace of Westphalia

Elizabeth I

Act of Uniformity

Armada

witchcraft craze

Thirty Years' War

absolutism

Louis XIV

Cardinal Richelieu

Cardinal Mazarin

Versailles

mercantilism

Prussia

Brandenburg

Frederick William the Great Elector

Austria

Russia

Muscovy

Ivan IV the Terrible

tsar

Romanov dynasty

Peter the Great

westernization

St. Petersburg

constitutional monarchy

James I

Puritans

Charles I and parliament

Oliver Cromwell

Restoration

Test Act

Glorious Revolution

William and Mary

Toleration Act

Thomas Hobbes

John Locke

Mannerism

El Greco

Baroque

Peter Paul Rubens

Bernini

Poussin

Elizabethan Era

William Shakespeare

Lope de Vega

Cervantes

Molière

III. Mapwork

Map 15.1. Catholics and Protestants in Europe by 1560

What distinguished the Anglican, Calvinist, and Lutheran reforms from each other?

Which countries resisted reform most strongly? Why?

How did the presence of reform affect political conflicts and alliances in sixteenth-century Europe?

Map 15.2 Europe in the Seventeenth Century

Which of the states in seventeenth-century Europe were absolutist in its government? Where did constitutional monarchy exist?

What are the differences between these two types of government?

What arguments do Thomas Hobbes and John Locke present in favor of these two systems?

IV. Datework

Chapter Timeline: From Martin Luther's Ninety-five Theses to the Reign of Peter the Great

How were the French Wars of Religion a consequence of the work of Martin Luther, John Calvin, and other Reformers?

What were the reformist responses to Protestantism within the Catholic church?

Why is the reign of Louis XIV considered an excellent example of absolutism in practice?

Chronology: Key Events of the Reformation Era

How did Pope Leo X respond to Luther's Ninety-five Theses? Why? What was the result for Catholicism?

What did the Jesuits contribute to the Catholic reformation? The Council of Trent?

Why did the popes ultimately acknowledge the need for reform? In which areas was reform undertaken? Which popes were especially involved?

Why is the Act of Supremacy an important step within the English Reformation?

Chronology: Europe in Crisis, 1560-1650: Key Events

Why was Philip II of Spain granted the honorary title "Most Catholic of Kings"?

What was the purpose of the Armada? Why did it fail? How was Queen Elizabeth I of England affected by this mission?

Briefly describe the importance of the following for European history: the Edict of Nantes, and the Peace of Westphalia. How do both religious and political issues determine these settlements? Why is it difficult to separate religious and political issues in this period?

Chronology: Absolute and Limited Monarchy

Why did Louis XIV revoke the Edict of Nantes? What was the result for the Huguenots?

What policies and practices distinguished an absolute ruler from a constitutional monarch?

Why did the Bill of Rights fail to settle the religious upheavals of seventeenth-century England?

V. Primary Sourcework

Protestant Reformation Primary Sources:

Luther and the Ninety-Five Theses: Selections

What reflection do you see here of Luther's original concern for salvation? For the practice of indulgences? Briefly explain that practice.

Do you see evidence here of Luther's belief in Justification through faith alone? For the sole authority of the Bible?

How does this document, especially in its statements about the pope, explain what happened at the Diet of Worms?

A Reformation Debate: The Marburg Colloquy, 1529

Why were Zwingli and Luther unable to agree on the meaning of the Last Supper?

What evidence does this debate excerpt provide for the supremacy of scriptural authority in Protestant reformers' thought?

Who do you think is winning this portion of the debate? Why?

A Protestant Woman: Catherine Zell to Ludwig Rabus of Memmingen

Why were the Anabaptists persecuted by both Catholics and Protestants?

How does Catherine Zell present herself as a model sixteenth-century Christian woman?

Seventeenth-Century Primary Sources:

A Witchcraft Trial in France: The Trial of Suzanne Gaudry

Why were women, particularly older women, especially vulnerable to accusations of witchcraft?

What "proofs" are offered here that Suzanne Gaudry had consorted with the devil?

Why was she executed, rather than merely punished, for her supposed crimes?

Peter the Great Deals with a Rebellion: Peter and the Streltsy

Why would an Austrian author of the seventeenth century be especially interested in the activities of Peter the Great?

Why was this tsar full of "curiosity of rambling abroad"? What changes did he initiate in Russia as a result of his travels?

The Bill of Rights

Why was the "Glorious Revolution" so called? What fears prompted it?

What rights are being granted to the parliament by the parliament in this document? Why did William and Mary allow this?

William Shakespeare: In Praise of England, from *Richard II*

Why is William Shakespeare aptly described as not merely a playwright, but a "complete man of the theatre"?

Why is English literature of the late sixteenth and early seventeenth centuries termed "Elizabethan"? What elements characterize the literature of this period in england?

Which countries might Shakespeare have meant to suggest by the phrase "...the envy of less happier lands"?

What details in the passage might suggest allusion to the Armada?

French Comedy: *The Would-Be Gentleman* by Jean-Baptiste Moliére

Whom does Moliére satirize in this play? Whom did he satirize in *Tartuffe* and with what result?

What observations of court life at Versailles are implicit here? What is the playwright satirizing about the acquisition of status in the French society of his day?

VI. Artwork

Art of the Protestant Reformation:

Woodcut: Luther versus the Pope

Why did state authorities support Luther?

How are the sentiments of Modern Devotion expressed here?

Why would this work of art appeal to the peasant class of Germany? What role did Luther's work play in the Peasants' War?

Charles V

What happened to Luther at the Diet of Worms? Why? What role did Charles V play?

What was the significance of the Peace of Augsburg for the Reformation? Why did Charles V negotiate this peace settlement?

John Calvin

Why was the Christian humanist Erasmus, unlike John Calvin, unwilling to become a reformer?

What did Calvin achieve with the *Institutes of the Christian Religion*?

How did Calvin build upon the earlier work of Zwingli?

Art of the Catholic Reformation:

Ignatius Loyola

What role did the Jesuits play in the Catholic reformation?

What values were especially important to the Jesuits? How was this order structured?

Sixteenth-Century Art

The Persecution of Witches

How were beliefs about witchcraft associated with medieval concerns with heresy?

Why were witchcraft crazes more common in areas affected by the Protestant Reformation?

Louis XIV

Why did Louis XIV call himself "The Sun King"? How is his choice of words revealing of his person?

Who were the chief ministers of Louis XIII and XIV? How did these men contribute to the power of the French monarchy?

Palace of Versailles

Why did Louis XIV establish a residence at Versailles and house his nobles for such long periods of time there?

What was Jean-Baptiste Colbert's role in the financing of Versailles?

How did France's policy of mercantilism allow the king to build on such a lavish scale?

Peter the Great

The Russian word "tsar" is related to the Latin name "Caesar." Who was the first Russian monarch to take this title? What image did Russian rulers create by assuming that ancient title?

Which other states in Europe were engaged in the development of strong military powers in the seventeenth century? Which were on the wane?

Execution of Charles I

With whom has the artist sympathized in this painting, the monarchy or Cromwell? How do you know?

Which English groups tended to favor the parliamentary radicals? Why?
Which favored the monarchy? Why?

Were the Puritans a part of this conflict?

Mannerist Art:

El Greco, *Laocöon*

What are the distinguishing characteristics of Mannerist art? How is this movement a reaction to the art of the High Renaissance?

What features of Mannerism are present in this painting?

Baroque Art:

Peter Paul Rubens, *The Landing of Marie de' Medici at Marseilles*

Compare this painting with the previous *Laocöon* of El Greco. How does Baroque painting represent a departure from Mannerism?

What elements of the Baroque style do you detect in this painting?

Who was the patron of this painting? Who was a patron of Fian Lorenzo Bernini? How do such patterns of patronage reflect the political realities of seventeenth-century Europe?

Nicholas Poussin, *Landscape with the Burial of Phocian*

What evidence does this painting provide for the retention of the High Renaissance style among French painters of the second half of the seventeeth century?

Why is this style known as French Classicism?

VII. Identifying Important Concepts Behind the Conclusion

The Conclusion to this chapter recalls the following key ideas:

1. Protestant and Catholic Reformations

2. European political conflicts and consequent rise of absolutist rulers and constitutional monarchy

3. Seventeenth-century European art and literature

Review these general concepts before moving on to the next chapter.

Chapter Sixteen: The Muslim Empires

I. Outlining the Chapter

Ottoman Empire
- Expansion of the Empire
    - Turkish Expansion in Europe
- Nature of Turkish Rule
- Religion and Society in the Ottoman World
- Ottomans in Decline
- Ottoman Art

Safavids
- Safavid Politics and Society
- Safavid Art and Literature

Grandeur of the Mughals
- Mughal Dynasty: A "Gunpowder Empire"?
- Akbar and Indo-Muslim Civilization
- Twilight of the Mughals
- Impact of Western Power in India
- Society and Culture under the Mughals
    - Daily Life
    - Mughal Culture

Conclusion

II. Terms and Persons To Know

Ottoman Turks

Orkhan I

Constantinople

beys

sultan

Murad I

Janissaries

Bayazid I

Mongols

Mehmet II

Istanbul

Selim I

pashas

Suleyman I the Magnificent

"gunpowder empires"

Topkapi Palace

harem

devshirme

viziers

sipahis

caliph

Sunni and Shi'ite Muslims

millet

causes for decline of Ottoman empire

mosques

Hagia Sophia

dome

decorative arts

Uzbecs

Safavid dynasty

Shah Ismail

Shah Abbas

Shah Hussein

Nadir Shah Afshar

Zand dynasty

amirs

Safavid Iran

Isfahan

art

Riza-i-Abbasi

literature

Mughal India

Babur

Humayun

Akbar

religious tolerance

Divine Faith

zamindars

Shah Jahan

Taj Mahal

Aurangzeb

decline of Mughal empire

European trade interests

English factories

East India Company

Joseph François Dupleix

Sir Robert Clive

Haidar Ali

British expansion

women

architecture

Humayun's mausoleum

painting

"Akbar style"

literature

Persian and Urdu

devotional literature

Tulsidas

Ramcaritmanas

Rajasthani painting

III. Mapwork

Map 16.1. The Ottoman Empire

Who was the founder of the Ottoman empire? From where did the Turkic-speaking peoples originally come? What religious values were spread by the extension of Ottoman power?

Who were the major competitors to the early Ottomans? Who represented the greatest threat to their power in the seventeenth century?

What role did the Janissaries play in the Ottoman empire? How did their presence balance the military forces organized by sultans and beys?

Map 16.2. The Ottoman and Safavid Empires, ca. 1683

Why do some scholars considered the Ottoman empire to have been a "gunpowder empire"? What does this term mean? Why is it used to describe the Safavid and Mughal empires as well?

Map 16.3. The Mughal Empire

Briefly describe the contributions of the following rulers of the Mughal dynasty: Babur, Humayun, and Akbar. How far did Akbar extend the territories he inherited?

Which Europeans were the first to establish a presence in India under the Mughals?

How did European, especially British, trade and industry contribute to the decline of this empire?

Map 16.4. India in 1805

Why did the Dutch and Portuguese ultimately cede India to British interests? Why did the French? How did the British acquire Bombay?

What interests of the English East India Company motivated British conquest of India?

IV. Datework

Chapter Timeline: From the Capture of Constantinople by the Ottoman Turks to the Collapse of the Safavid Empire

Identify the following eras on this timeline: Ottoman empire, Safavid empire, and the reign of the Mughal dynasty in India.

What did the term "shah" mean when it was used by Persian rulers? What achievements of Shah Ismail, Abbas and Jahan reflect the various implications of this title?

Chronology: The Ottoman Empire

Why was Constantinople so important to Ottoman aspirations? What plans did Orkhan I and Mehmet II have for the city? What was the city called after 1453?

Into what regions did Selim and Suleyman I expand the Ottoman empire? What oppostion did they encounter?

How did the Ottoman presence transform the countries that came under Turkish rule?

Chronology: The Safavids

Why did the Safavids claim supremacy and orthodoxy in contrasting themselves with the Ottomans? What conflicts resulted from these claims?

Why was Shah Abbas I known as "Abbas the Great"? What was his relationship to the prophet Muhammad?

What political, military, and economic measures did the shahs of Persia use to efficiently run their empire? What special authority accompanied the title of shah?

Chronology: The Mughal Era

What era is initiated by the arrival of Vasco da Gama at Calicut? How do the Jesuit missions, the foundation of English and French territories in India, and the Battle of Plassey, all derive from that initial event?

What role did Empress Nur Jahan play in the transition of Mughal rule from Jahangir to Shah Jahan?

Why was Madras especially desired by the French?

V. Primary Sourcework

Ottoman Primary Sources:

The Fall of Constantinople: Kritovoulos, *Life of Mehmed the Conqueror*

How did the Byzantines attempt to defend their city from the forces of Mehmet II? Why did these efforts fail?

How does this Greek author depict the Turkish sultan?

Why does Kritovoulos say that the soldiers attacked the citizens of Constantinople? What other motivations are possible?

A Portrait of Suleyman the Magnificent: Ghislain de Busbecq, *The Turkish Letters*

Busbecq states that his message to the Sultan "did not correspond with his [Suleyman's] expectations." Why? What expectations might the Sultan have had in regard to the Habsburg rulers?

What evidence does this document provide for the harem system in Turkish courts? For the difficulties in succession?

A Turkish Discourse on Coffee: Katib Chelebi, *The Balance of Truth*

From where did the Turkish first import coffee? What other products became popular in Turkish culture at this time?

What prohibitive measures did Turkish rulers attempt to impose on the trade and drinking of coffee? Why did these fetwas and measures fail?

Mughal Primary Sources:

The Mughal Conquest of North India: Babur, *Memoirs*

Locate Agra on map 16.3. How far did Babur extend his empire from this point? How did he enrich this city after his victory?

To what does Babur attribute his success in warfare? What religious view is he expressing here?

An Elephant Fight for the King's Entertainment: François Bernier, *Travels in the Mogul Empire*

Why does Bernier say that elephants had become less useful in warfare?

Why would Mughal emperors have sponsored fights of this kind? How did such an exhibition reflect on the ruler and his court?

A Description of Hindustan: Babur, *Memoirs*

In spite of its faults in Emperor Babur's eyes, why did he value Hindustân enough to conquer it?

What implicit reference to the caste system does the emperor make in this passage? Why has he found its existence convenient?

The Uses of the Coconut: Duarte Barbosa, *The Book of Duarte Barbosa*

How did the use of leaves "as paper," noted here by Barbosa, affect the early history of Indian painting?

Why does Barbosa call the Indians "the Heathen"?

Why would this Portuguese official describe the coconut in such detail? To what purposes might this document have been put?

VI. Artwork

Ottoman Art:

The Turkish Conquest of Constantinople

How is the actual geographic position of Constantinople reflected in this painting? How are the factual events of the seige presented? What elements of fantasy are included?

Is this painting the visual equivalent of a document such as the preceding account by Kritovoulos of the sack of Constantinople? Is one historical source superior to the other? Why or why not?

Mehmet II, Conquerer of Constantinople

Which art forms came to a particularly advanced level under the patronage of the Ottoman rulers?

Why would the Ottoman sultan wish to be depicted in this manner? Does this painting provide any indication of Mehmet's military accomplishments? Why or why not?

Inside a Turkish Mosque

How did the original form of the prayer halls in a Turkish mosque differ from the later mosques modelled after Hagia Sophia? How did they both differ from the original outdoor sites for prayer?

Why was this change desirable? What economic factors allowed such a dramatic change from simple open-air courtyards?

How do such changes compare with historical changes in Christian architecture?

Safavid Art:

The Royal Academy of Isfahan

Why would theological schools have been such an important component of Safavid Islamic culture? Why would literacy have been valued so highly?

What architectural references does this building make to the mosque form? Why are the surfaces of the arcades decorated with arabesques? What other Islamic arts made wide use of arabesque patterns?

Two Lovers

What were the characteristics of Persian painting drawn upon by Safavid painters? How does this work both use and transform those earlier traditions?

Why is Safavid painting considered superior to Safavid poetry?

Mughal Art:

Akbar Restrains an Elephant

How does this pair of paintings compliment Akbar? Why is he shown disobeying his chief minister? Disregarding his own safety?

Where has the artist placed Akbar's men? Why is this significant?

The Palace of the Winds at Jaipur

How does the Palace of the Winds reflect Mughal adoption of Muslim practices, especially in regard to women?

What similarities do you perceive between this facade the the facades of earlier Hindu temples in India? What important difference has occured in the intricate carved designs?

The Taj Mahal

What architectural references does the Taj Mahal make to the mosque form? Why? Where did this style of tomb originate?

How is this building involved in the story of Shah Jahan's death? What does this story contribute to our understanding of succesion to the throne in the Mughal period? How were such problems similar to those encountered by the Ottoman sultans? By the Safavid shahs?

Fatehpur Sikri

What does the combination of the Sufi mystical inspiration for Fatehpur Sikri, and its inclusion of a mosque, indicate about Indian religious practices during the reign of Akbar?

What other artistic achievements illuminated his reign?

VII. Identifying Important Concepts Behind the Conclusion

The Conclusion to this chapter recalls the following key ideas:

1. Ottoman empire

2. Safavid empire

3. Mughal empire

Review these general concepts before moving on to the next chapter.

Chapter Seventeen: The East Asian World

I. Outlining the Chapter

China at Its Apex
- From the Ming to the Qing
  - First Contacts with the West
  - Ming Brought to Earth
- Greatness of the Qing
  - Qing Politics
  - China on the Eve of the Western Onslaught
- Changing China
  - Population Explosion
  - Seeds of Industrialization
- Daily Life in Qing China
  - Family
  - Role of Women
- Cultural Developments
  - Rise of the Chinese Novel
  - Theater and Popular Drama
  - Art of the Ming and the Qing

Tokugawa Japan
- Three Great Unifiers
- Opening to the West
- Tokugawa "Great Peace"
  - Life in the Village
- Tokugawa Culture
  - Literature of the New Middle Class
  - Tokugawa Art

Korea: The Hermit Kingdom

Conclusion

II. Terms and Persons To Know

Chinese Empire and the West

Marco Polo and Khubilai Khan

Confucian institutions

hierarchy of officials

decline of Chinese trade

Portuguese

Jesuits

Decline of Ming dynasty

Manchus

Li Zicheng

Qing dynasy

Koxinga

Kangxi

Yongzheng

Qianlong

dyarchy

quotas

"Sacred Edict"

"Textual Criticism"

Heshen

White Lotus Rebellion

Russia

kowtow

Amur River

English

East India Company

imperial controls on European trade

Lord Macartney

King George III and Qianlong

Yangtze River

population increase

industrialization

controls on native commerce

clocks

"five relationships"

joint family

clan

women

foot-binding

Chinese novel

Monkey

The Golden Lotus

The Dream of the Red Chamber

drama

The Peony Pavilion

popular theatre

"Forbidden City"

Ming and Qing arts

daimyo

Oda Nobunaga

Toyotomi Hideyoshi

Korea

unification of Japan

Tokugawa Ieyasu

shogun

Portuguese

Francis Xavier

eviction of missionaries

Japanese controls on European trade

bakufu

shogunate government

hostage system

samurai

expansion of trade and manufacturing

Edo

ronin

rural unrest

village life

Saikaku

kabuki

"floating world"

bunraku

Chikamatsu

Basho

hokku

painting

Tohaku

woodblock print

Utamaro

Hokusai

Hiroshige

Yi dynasty

Yi Song Gye

yangban

chonmin

hangul

policy of isolation

Manchu invasion

III. Mapwork

Map 17.1. China and Its Enemies during the Late Ming Era

Who are the northern peoples identified on this map as the Jurchen? How were their incursions into China different from those of the Mongols?

Why was Canton such an important site for European trade? How did Chinese emperors use this city to maintain strict divisions between Europeans and native Chinese peoples?

Which Japanese ruler aspired to attack China? How did Korea enter into this conflict?

Map 17.2. The Qing Empire in the Eighteenth Century

How did the existence of the "Little Brothers" or tributary states depicted on this map form Chinese expectations about the emerging Chinese-European trade relationship?

Why were these expectations on the part of the "Celestial Court" unable to be realized?

Map 17.3. Tokugawa Japan

Why did Tokugawa Ieyasu lay seige to Osaka? Why thereafter does Edo become the most important and flourishing city in Japan?

Which cities were open to European traders? Under what conditions? What was the European response to such limits?

How far is mainland China from Japan? The Korean peninsula? How is this proximity important to an understanding Japanese history?

IV. Datework

Chapter Timeline: From the Invention of a Phonetic Alphabet for the Korean Language to the White Lotus Rebellion in China

What changes did Koreans make that demonstrated a growing independence from Chinese cultural domination? In terms of writing, why was *hangul* originally despised by the *yangban*?

What factors enabled the Manchus to take control of China? Exactly when did this occur? What governmental policies distinguished them from the earlier foreign people who ruled this country, the Mongols?

How long did Manchu domination last? Which dynasty included Manchu rulers? Among them, why is Kanxgi considered by some scholars to have been the greatest ruler in Chinese history?

Chronology: China During the Early Modern Era

Locate Taiwan on Map 17.1. How was this base an important complement to trading from Canton? What is the history of European use of this island?

What commonalities do you preceive between the seventeenth-century uprising led by Li Zicheng and the White Lotus Rebellion approximately a century and a half later? What issues continued to plague China? Why?

Why did LiZicheng begin his revolt? How did his capture of Beijing lead to the seizure of China by the Manchus?

Why did Koxinga expel the Dutch from Taiwan?

Chronology: Japan and Korea During the Early Modern Era

How did Portuguese merchants first arrive in Japan?

What does the Jesuit missionary Francis Xavier accomplish in Japan?

Why are Oda Nobunaga, Toyotomi Hideyoshi, and Tokugawa Ieyasu considered the three great unifiers of Japan? How does each build upon the achievements of his predecessors?

Who were the *ronin*? What does their existence demonstrate about the changing role of the samurai in early modern Japan?

V. Primary Sourcework

Qing Primary Source:

The Tribute System in Action: A Decree of Emperor Qianlong

Why was King George III so displeased by this letter from Qianlong? In fact, what did he say when he read the Chinese emperor's response?

Who has the "Celestial Court" allowed into China? Into Peking? Under what conditions? Why?

What actions did England take as a result of Qianlong's rejection of English interests in China?

Primary Source for the Ming:

The Art of Printing: Matteo Ricci, *The Diary of Matthew Ricci*

Why were the Jesuits so active in China? Were their missionary activities successful? Why were they eventually expelled?

What evidence does this document provide for the Jesuit practice of adapting to native customs? Why was their policy of limited conformity wise? Why was it severely criticized by some other Christian groups?

Qing Primary Sources:

A Confucian Sixteen Commandments: Kangxi's Sacred Edict

What similarities do you perceive between Kangxi's Confucian edict and the Tokugawa decree that follows later in the chapter? Why would such similarities exist?

What did Emperor Kangxi hope to achieve by issuing a "Sacred Edict" on Confucianism? Why did other Confucian scholars continue to oppose him?

Why would general obedience to these commandments make the emperor's task of governance an easier one? Which laws in particular are aimed at securing cooperation with government officials?

The Art of Using Chopsticks: *The Dream of the Red Chamber*

What class prejudices in Chinese society are reflected in this passage? How are such differences between rural and urban, and upper and peasant classes, important for understanding life in China during the Qing dynasty?

What characteristic features of the popular Chinese novel are evident in this passage from Qing fiction? Why is its author unknown?

Japanese Primary Sources:

A Present for Lord Tokitaka: The Japanese Discover Firearms

How does Lord Tokitaka apply the teachings of Lao Tzu to the use of firearms?

What evidence do you see here for the adaptation of the Portuguese traders to Japanese ways of thinking and speaking? How is this successful trade strategy similar to the missionary strategies employed by the Jesuits?

What will be the consequences of Tokitaka's "experiments" for the history of Japan?

Toyotomi Hideyoshi Expels the Missionaires: Letter to the Viceroy of the Indies

Why did Hideyoshi consider Christianity to consist of "wrong, unreasonable and wanton doctrines"? How had the behavior of missionaries in Japan convinced him of this idea?

What similarities exist between Buddhism, Confucianism, and Shinto, that lead Hideyoshi to write that "To know Shinto is to know Buddhism as well as Confucianism"? Why is Christianity not included?

How does Hideyoshi explain his success in governance? What were his plans in regard to Korea and "the great Ming nation"?

Following the Straight and Narrow in Tokugawa Japan: Maxims for Peasant Behavior

Who comprised the *bakufu* under the Japanese shogunate? Why is the maintenance of social order paramount to their interests?

Would obedience to these provisions have contributed to the peasant standard of living and quality of life, or not? Why?

What Confucian elements in the earlier Sacred Edit of the Chinese Emperor Kangxi are lacking in this Japanese decree?

How is concern for the *ie* expressed in this document? What similarities do you perceive between such concern and the fundamental structures of Chinese society (the joint family and clan)?

Korean Primary Source:

Waste Not, Want Not: A Korean Presceiption for Prosperity

Do you suppose that this Neo-Confucian philosopher's advice to the Korean monarch was warmly received? Why would the ruler have maintained advisors versed in Chinese intellectual traditions at his court?

What concerns for the peasantry and *chonmin* are evident here? How did the *yangban* benefit from their existence?

VI. Artwork

Ming Art:

World Class China Ware

What does the Dutch word "kraak" reveal about competitive trading practices by European nations in the East?

Why did trade by both the Silk Road and by sea decline under the Ming? Did this change during the Qing dynasty?

Tibetan Art:

The Potala Palace in Tibet

What policies of expansion by the Qing brought Tibet under that dynasty's influence? What other regions were similarly affected?

In the seventeenth century, was Buddhism the dominant religion in China? What beliefs and rituals were most important to the Chinese under the Ming and Qing?

Qing Art:

Sweating Out Exam Results

How did Manchu employment of quotas and the dyarchy system affect Chinese attainment of civil service positions?

Why were official posts so increasingly difficult to obtain? What attempts were made by the aristocratic class to make positions more available to them?

Emperor Qianlong Meets Lord Macartney

What was Lord Macartney refusing to do when he refused to kowtow to Qianlong? Why did he refuse to perform this ritual? Was this merely an issue of etiquette? What compromise was reached on this matter?

Why were Western scientific instruments and texts greeted with less interest and enthusiasm than the British had expected? What beliefs are thus revealed on both sides of the exchange?

Ming and Qing architecture:

The Imperial City in Beijing

Which emperor originally built a palace on this site? For how long did it remain the imperial city?

What arts flourished within these walls?

What prohibitions were placed on Chinese commoners and all Europeans in regard to the city? Why were such provisions considered necessary for both groups?

Japanese Art and Architecture:

The Siege on Osaka Castle

After the seige on Osaka, where did Tokugawa Ieyasu locate his capital?

Why is the Tokugawa period in Japan sometimes referred to as the "Great Peace"?

What domestic and foreign policies maintained Tokugawa governance of a unified Japan?

The Portuguese Arrive at Nagasaki

How are the Portuguese distinguished from the Japanese in this painting? How is their purpose in coming to Japan made clear?

What products were traded by the Portuguese in Japan? What religious conflicts resulted from their presence?

Is an entire historical narrative being told in this painting, or a single event? What features of the work support your answer?

A Japanese Castle

What part did the daimyo play in the shogunate governance of Japan?

How did the shogunate employ the "hostage system" to control the influence of powerful samurai warriors?

On the other hand how did widespread "sword hunts" serve to maintain the position of the samurai over the common people?

The Floating World of Edo

Consider this print along with the previous source document on "Following the Straight and Narrow in Tokugawa Japan." With such rigid rules prescribed for village life, why was "the floating world" allowed to exist in the city?

What role did *kabuki* and *bunraku* play in urban life during the Tokugawa period?

Korean Architecture:

Seoul Palace Pagoda

What effect did Toyotomi Hideyoshi and the Qing dynasty have on Korea?

How did the Yi dynasty come into power in Korea? Who was the founder of this dynasty? Under the Yi, why might Korea be described as "the hermit kingdom"?

VII. Identifying Important Concepts Behind the Conclusion

The Conclusion to this chapter recalls the following key ideas:

1. China during the Ming and Qing dynasties

2. Japan during the Sixteenth, Seventeenth, and Eighteenth centuries, especially the Tokugawa shogunate

Review these general concepts, and the closing section on Korea, before moving on to the next chapter.

Chapter Eighteen
Toward a New Heaven and a New Earth: An Intellectual Revolution in the West

I. Outlining the Chapter

Scientific Revolution
- Background to the Scientific Revolution
- Toward a New Heaven: A Revolution in Astronomy
- Breakthrough in Medicine
- Women in the Origins of Modern Science
- Toward a New Earth: Descartes, Rationalism, and a New View of Humankind
- Science and Religion in the Seventeenth Century
- Spread of Scientific Knowledge

Enlightenment
- Paths to Enlightenment
- Philosophes and Their Ideas
    - Toward a New "Science of Man"
    - Later Enlightenment
    - "Woman's Question" in the Enlightenment
- Social Environment of the Philosophes

Culture and Society in an Age of Enlightenment
- Innovations in Art, Music, and Literature
- High Culture
- Popular Culture
- Crime and Punishment

Religion and the Churches
- Toleration and Religious Minorities
- Popular Religion in the Eighteenth Century

Conclusion

II. Terms and Persons To Know

Scientific Revolution

medieval worldview

Greek thinkers: Aristotle, Ptolemy, and Galen

Renaissance humanists

Renaissance artists

new instruments

mathematics

Hermeticism

Ptolemaic conception of the universe

Nicolaus Copernicus

On the Revolutions of the Heavenly Spheres

heliocentric conception of the universe

Johannes Kepler

Tycho Brahe

Galileo Galilei

The Starry Messenger

Roman Inquisition

Isaac Newton

Principia

three laws of motion

universal law of gravitation

Newtonian mechanistic concept

medicine

Galen

Andreas Vesalius

William Harvey

humanist education for women

female scientists

Margaret Cavendish

Maria Winkelmann

perpetuation of old stereotypes about women

René Descartes

Discourse on Method

Cartesian dualism

modern rationalism

conflict between science and religion

natural philosophers

growing secularization

Blaise Pascal

Pensées

Francis Bacon

The Great Instauration

inductive principles

English and French scientific societies

The Enlightenment

Immanuel Kant

reason

Bernard de Fontenelle

skepticism

travel literature

John Locke

Essay Concerning Human Understanding

tabula rasa

philosophes

Baron de Montesquieu

Voltaire

deism

Diderot

Encyclopedia

"science of man"

Physiocrats

laissez-faire

Adam Smith

The Wealth of Nations

Jean-Jacques Rousseau

The Social Contract and *Emile*

Mary Astell

Mary Wollstonecraft

Vindication of the Rights of Woman

salons

Marie-Thérèse de Geoffrin

learned and secret societies

Rococo art

Antoine Watteau

Giovanni Battista Tiepolo

Baroque-Rococo architectural style

Balthasar Neumann

Baroque musical style

Johann Sebastian Bach

George Frederick Handel

Classical musical style

Franz Joseph Haydn

Wolfgang Amadeus Mozart

English novel

Samuel Richardson

Henry Fielding

high culture

popular culture

Carnival

punishments for crimes

religious toleration

Ashkenazic Jews

Sephardic Jews

Joseph II

religious devotion

confraternities

"rational Christianity"

Methodism

John Wesley

III. Mapwork

Map 18.1. The Age of the Enlightenment in Europe

What factors enabled the Enlightenment to become not merely a national movement, but an international one? Which countries contributed most to the development and spread of Enlightenment discoveries and values?

Why were secular governments and church authorities divided over the importance of the Enlightenment? Why did Enlightenment thinkers proceed anyway? Who ultimately triumphed in this debate? What were the consequences, even up to the present day, for Western societies?

Why was the Enlightenment so called? How does this movement relate to the Scientific Revolution? Is it identical with it?

Does this European concept of the Enlightenment bear any resemblance to the Hindu concept of enlightenment, or Nirvana?

IV. Datework

Chapter Timeline: From Copernicus' *On the Revolutions of the Heavenly Spheres* to the Close of the Eighteenth Century

How did Renaissance humanism, art, and magic lay the foundations for the Scientific Revolution of the sixteenth through eighteenth centuries in Europe?

Why was the *Encyclopedia* of Diderot so important to the spread of Enlightenment ideas? How does this relate to the work of Fontanelle? To the salons?

How did the Baroque muscial style, exemplified in the compositions of Bach and Handel, differ from the Classical music of Haydn and Mozart which followed it?

Chronology: Important Works of the Scientific Revolution

Describe the relation between the following two pairs of works: Copernicus' *On the Revolutions of the Heavenly Spheres* and Galileo's *The Starry Messenger*, and Vesalius' *On the Fabric of the Human Body* and Harvey's *On the Motion of the Heart and Blood.* In each pair, how did the work of the later scientist draw upon the discoveries of the former?

What significance does Newton's *Principia* have for the Scientific Revolution? Did Newton believe in God? Why was this considered an important question? How was his mechanistic model of the universe employed after his death in the church-science controversy? What features of his cosmology are expressed by the development of deism?

Chronology: Works of the *Philosophes*

How did the works of Diderot, along with those of Fontanelle, spread the ideas of the Scientific Revolution outside a limited intellectual circle?

Why is Smith's *Wealth of Nations* considered a classic argument for *laissez-faire* economic policy? What did Smith believe were the advantages of economic liberalism?

How does the concepts of "natural law" and "natural man" underly Montesquieu's masterwork *The Spirit of the Laws*? Rousseau's *Emile*? What do these terms mean?

V. Primary Sourcework

Primary Sources of the Scientific Revolution in Europe:

On the Revolutions of the Heavenly Spheres, Nicolaus Copernicus

How did Copernicus' model of the universe differ from the model prevalent in his day? From where was this medieval conception derived?

This document reveals that the idea that the earth moves was not original to Copernicus. Since it was not, why did it seem so "absurd" to sixteenth-century authorities? To what authors does Copernicus attribute the original idea? When did these scientists live? What reflection of Renaissance humanism is reflected in his use of these sources?

What consequences did Copernicus' publication of this work have for Copernicus himself? For the Catholic Church? For the history of astronomy? For science in general?

The Starry Messenger, Galileo Galilei

What was the response of the Roman Inquisition to the publication of *The Starry Messenger*?

Why did the Inquisition, founded to battle heresies, concern itself with Galileo's scientific findings and publications? Why were they especially disturbed by features such as the "chains of mountains and deep valleys" Galileo reports seeing on the moon in this passage?

Why does Galileo mention "philosophy" and "philosophers" in this passage? Does he mean these terms in the original sense (according to the original ancient Greek conception)?

What were the long-term consequences for the relation between science and the church in the West?

The Father of Modern Rationalism: René Descartes, *Discourse on Method*

Given the history of medieval-based approaches to science in the West, why does Descartes express such strong determination in this passage "to accept nothing as true which I did not evidently know to be such"?

What is Cartesian dualism? Why are reason and the tool of mathematics paramount for human progress in this conception of the world?

According to Descartes, what was the role of God in the nature of the universe?

Why were Descartes' books placed on the Index of Forbidden Books?

The Attack on Religious Intolerance: Voltaire, *The Ignorant Philosopher* and *Candide*

What criticisms does Voltaire make against religious fanaticism in this passage? Did the skeptics believe that religion could exist without such negative consequences?

Why would a minister's wife want Candide to denounce the Pope as the Antichrist? What statement about religious factionalism is Voltaire making here?

How did eighteenth-century travel literature contribute to the religious skepticism of many *philosophes*?

Diderot Questions Christian Sexual Standards: Denis Diderot, *Supplement to the Voyage of Bougainville*

Why did Diderot term Christianity "the most absurd and most atrocious in its dogma" of all religions?

What similarities do you perceive between this work and the *Persian Letters* of Montesquieu? Why was such a format well-suited to enlightenment criticism?

Why is Western morality, but not the Western stereotype for women, not considered here?

The Rights of Women: Mary Wollstonecraft, *Vindication of the Rights of Woman*

By what means did Wollstonecraft propose that women could become "better citizens"? What would be the positive results for both women and men?

What picture does the author paint of the women of her day? Why are they in such a deplorable state? How does Wollstonecraft suggest that both women and men are at fault for the "slavish" situation of females?

Why did Enlightenment learned societies exclude women? How was "scientific" anatomy used to perpetuate old sterotypes about women?

Eighteenth-Century Primary Sources:

The Punishment of Crime: Restif de la Bretonne, *Nocturnal Spectator: The Broken Man*

Why were punishments meted out to criminals in the eighteenth century in plain view of the public?

How did Carnival contribute to crime? Where did Carnival fall in the church calendar?

What positive acts on the part of the church does the author commend in this passage?

The Conversion Experience in Wesley's Methodism: *The Works of the Reverend John Wesley*

In this excerpt from Wesley's diary, how does the Methodist preacher describe the conversion experiences he presides over? How did his own experience provide a model for his work?

Were such violent events a part of Catholic or Anglican worship? Why?

VI. Artwork

Art of the Scientic Revolution and Enlightenment:

The Medieval Conception of the Universe and the Copernican System

In the medieval conception of the universe shown here, the outer sphere is identified in Latin as the "heavenly empire, the dwelling of God and of all the saved souls." In Copernicus' plan, the outer sphere is titled the "immobile sphere of the fixed stars." In respect to these outer spheres, how does Copernicus' conception differ significantly from the medieval model? How is it the same? What does the sameness reveal about Copernicus' conservatism?

Galileo's Sketch of the Phases of the Moon

Did Galileo invent the telescope? (See also the following primary source reading from *The Starry Messenger.*) How was his invention related to the Flemish "spyglass"?

Why did Galileo's discoveries of material substances and formations on the moon strongly refute the traditional medieval cosmology current in his day? Why did his discoveries stun contemporary religious authorites?

Descartes with Queen Christina of Sweden

What were the consequences of the triumph of Cartesian dualism for Western thought?

What role did women play in addition to royal patronage of the type this painting documents? What contributions were made by Winkelmann in the area of astronomy? How did Astell and Wollstonecraft enter the debate on women's opportunities?

Louis XIV and Colbert Visit the Academy of Sciences

How did the leading French and English learned societies differ in the seventeenth and eighteenth centuries? How were these differences reflected in the academies' membership and funding?

How do these differences reflect the structures of the French and English polticial systems?

Why were monarchs such as Louis XIV interested in the progress of learned societies?

Voltaire

What does the term *philosophe* mean? What was the role of such a person in Enlightenment society? Why do some scholars consider Voltaire to have been the most important of the *philosophes*?

Briefly explain the importance of Voltaires' *Treatise on Toleration.*

The Salon of Madame Geoffrin

Did the work of Winkelmann, the writings of Astell and Wollstonecraft, or the salons of Madame Geoffrin change current perceptions about females? Why or why not? How were each of these women's efforts different?

Rococo Art:

Antoine Watteau, *The Pilgrimage to Cythera*

What lyrical qualities do you perceive in this Rococo painting? Are there elements of sadness present? What other characteristics of the Rococo does this painting exemplify?

How did the Rococo represent a departure from Baroque art?

Why would Enlightenment artistocratic tastes have been pleased by this painting's reference to Greek mythology rather than to a Christian theme?

Baroque-Rococo Architecture:

Vierzehnheiligen, Exterior View

What Baroque and Rococo elements are evident in Neumann's church facade?

Consider this architectural style in light of Map 18.1. Why were monarchs of Europe eager to imitate the Palace of Versailles? Which courts were able to build palaces in the Baroque-Rococo style?

Eighteenth Century Art:

John Wesley

What defects in English religious life did Wesley believe existed? How did he attempt to improve the English church?

What does the success of his "revival" demonstrate about popular religion in the eighteenth century as opposed to the intellectual movements described in this chapter? How does this split relate to differences in American society today?

VII. Identifying Important Concepts Behind the Conclusion

The Conclusion to this chapter recalls the following key ideas:

1. Scientific Revolution

2. Enlightenment

3. Eighteenth-century culture, art, literature, music, and religion

Review these general concepts before moving on to the next chapter.

Chapter Nineteen: Europe on the Eve of a New World Order

I. Outlining the Chapter

Economic Changes and the Persistence of a Traditional Social Order
- Population, Food, and Industry
- Worldwide Trade
- Society in the Eighteenth Century

Changing Patterns of War: Global Confrontation
- The Seven Years' War (1756-1763): A Global War
- European Armies and Warfare in the Eighteenth Century

Colonial Empires and Revolution
- Society of Latin America
  - Economic Foundations
  - State and Church in Colonial Latin America
- British North America
  - American Revolution and the Birth of a New Nation

Toward a New Political Order
- Background: Enlightened Absolutism in the Eighteenth Century
- French Revolution
  - From Discontent to the Destruction of the Old Regime
  - From Radical Revolution to Reaction
- Age of Napoleon
  - Napoleon's Empire and the European Response

Conclusion

II. Terms and Persons To Know

population growth

food

cottage industry

Richard Arkwright

global economy

European social organization

peasantry

nobles

townspeople

"balance of power"

"reason of state"

Silesia

Seven Years' War or French and Indian War

French and British North America

mercantilist theory

Gulf of St. Lawrence

Ohio River valley

William Pitt the Elder

General James Wolfe

Louis-Joseph Montcalm

Treaty of Paris

armies and navies

Portuguese and Spanish colonial empires

Latin America

mestizos

African slaves

multiracial society

precious metals

agriculture

repartimento

peons

haciendas and fazendas

raw materials

viceroy

Spanish administration of American empire

Spanish Bourbon kings

missions

Catholicism in Latin America

Sor Juana Inés de la Cruz

British North America

Parliament

Hanoverians

Robert Walpole

Stamp Act

voters

representation

national identity

First Continental Congress

Lexington and Concord

Second Continental Congress

Declaration of Independence

Thomas Jefferson

Continental Army

George Washington

French, Spanish, Dutch, and Russian support of colonies

Cornwallis

Treaty of Paris

Articles of Confederation

Constitution

"checks and balances"

three branches of federal government

Federalists

Bill of Rights

natural laws

natural rights

"enlightened absolutism"

Frederick William I

General Directory

Junkers

Prussian army

Frederick the Great

Austrian Empire

Joseph II

Catherine the Great

Instruction

Charter of the Nobility

Emelyan Pugachev

Russian territorial expansion

Three Estates of French society

bourgeoisie

Louis XVI

Estates-General

National Assembly

Bastille

popular uprisings

Great Fear

Declaration of the Rights of Man and the Citizen

Olympe de Gouges

Declaration of the Rights of Woman and the Female Citizen

Civil Constitution of the Clergy

revolutionary consensus

war with Austria

National Convention

execution of Louis XVI

Commune

European coalition against France

Committee of Public Safety

Maximilien Robespierre

Jacobins

"people's wars"

Reign of Terror

Lyons

dechristianization

Thermidorean Reaction

Directory

Napoleon Bonaparte

first consul

Emperor Napoleon I

Concordat

Napoleonic Civil Code

bureaucracy

new aristocracy

second European coalition

third coalition

Grand Empire

collapse of Grand Empire

Britain

nationalism

invasion of Russia

Louis XVIII

Waterloo

Duke of Wellington

III. Mapwork

Map 19.1. Global Trade Patterns of the European States in the Eighteenth Century

What were the most important raw materials and foods exported to Europe from the Americas in the Eighteenth Century? Along what boundary lines did the British and French divide North America? How did the Spanish and Portuguese crowns partition South America?

What trade in the East and West qualifies this system as a "global economy"?

Map 19.2. The Seven Years' War

Why did many Indians side with the French rather than the British in this war?

How were global wars different from preceding warfare? What qualifies the Seven Years' War as a global conflict? In this war, what conflicts occurred in Europe? Where did the Great War for Empire occur?

In contrast to the French Revolution, why is this conflict not termed a "people's war"?

What were the terms of the Treaty of Paris?

Map 19.3. Latin America in the Eighteenth Century

In the Spanich colonies, how was the *repartimento* system intended to improve upon the *encomienda* system? Did it work? Why or why not?

Who were the peons? Briefly explain the evolution of haciendas and fazendas in the Spanish and Portuguese American colonies.

Why did these colonies come to be called Latin America?

Map 19.4. North America, 1700-1803

Why did the French help the American colonists with their revolution against the British?

What territories were granted to the Americans by the Treaty of Paris in 1783?

What events in Russia and in Europe kept Russia from maintaining vast territories in the Americas in the eighteenth century?

Map 19.5. Europe in 1763

What is the history of the conflict over Austrian Silesia? Why did this relatively small area cause such devastating and lengthy conflicts?

Why did so many European powers enter into the Prussian Austrian dispute? Which played the most prominent roles? Why?

Map 19.6. Napoleon's Grand Empire

Where was Napoleon successful in extending French empire? How was he finally defeated?

How is Napoleon's vision of a threefold Grand empire reflected on this map? What three elements did he envision?

Locate on the map and consider the importance of the following in the life of Napoleon: Trafalgar, the Russian Invasion route, Elba, and Waterloo.

IV. Datework

Chapter Timeline: From Britain Participation in the Spanish American Market to the Battle of Waterloo

What ideas about enlightened government did Frederick the Great, Joseph II, and Catherine the Great put into action? Which succeeded? Which did not? Why? From where did these ideas originate?

What did Americans call the Seven Years' War? Why?

What policies of Robespierre, the National Convention and the Committee of Public Safety led to the Reign of Terror in France? How did it end?

Chronology: The European States--Enlightened Absolutism in the Eighteenth Century

What role did Prussian militarism play in eighteenth-century European politics?

What modern countries exist today in the region once known as Prussia?

How do the *Instruction* and Charter of the Nobility of Catherine the Great represent the changes her enlightened policies underwent during her thirty-four year reign?

How did Pugachev's rebellion affect the evolution of Catherine the Great's policies?

Chronology: The French Revolution

Why did Louis XVI call a session of the Estates-General in 1789? Why had that body not met since 1614?

How did the meeting of the Estates-General lead to the formation of a National Assembly? Why was this new assembly essentially illegal?

Why was the National Convention originally formed? How was it different from the earlier National Assembly?

Why did the National Convention give such broad powers to a Committee on Public Safety?

What was the Civil Constitution of the Clergy? Why did traditionally Catholic France pass such a decree? How did Napoleon's Concordat seek to make partial amends for this oath? For dechristianization?

Why was Robespierre executed?

Chronology: The Age of Napoleon, 1799-1815

How did the Concordat help to pacify France?

Why did Napoleon's Continental System fail?

Why did the exiled Napoleon return to Paris in 1815? What did he hope to accomplish at Waterloo?

V. Primary Sourcework

Eighteenth-Century European Primary Sources:

The Beginnings of Mechanized Industry: The Attack on New Machines, *The Yorkshire Cloth Workers' Petition (1786).*

What crisis did Richard Arkwright's "water loom" lead to in the English cottage industry of textile manufacturing?

According to this workers' petition, how many laborers did a single scribbling-machine replace?

What concerns did the workers have concerning the unemployed? Why do they mention children as part of this group?

Poverty in France: M. de la Bourdonnaye, Intendant of Bordeaux, to the Controller-General, September 30, 1708

Why did M. de la Bourdonnaye fear riots? How does his concern foreshadow the role the poor would play in the French Revolution?

What was the taille? Who was exempt from this obligation? Why? What provisions are made in this document for the poor in regard to the taille? Would these provisions be temporary or permanent? Why?

Primary Sources on the Americas:

Class and Caste in Colonial Latin America: George Juan and Antonio de Ulloa, *Voyage to South America*

Who were the creoles? The mestizos? The mulattoes? Why were such distinctions made in Latin American colonial society?

According to the authors, how were occupation and class tied to race? Why?

The Mission: Félix de Azara, *Description and History of Paraguay and Rio de la Plata*

How were the missions organized to enable missionaries to control many aspects of the Indians' lives? Why was this deemed necessary?

Why would the missionaries have forbidden the women to sew? What reference to mercantilism do you percieve in the last paragraph of the passage?

Russian Primary Source:

The Proposals of Catherine II for a New Law Code

What liberal ideas of the *philosophes* do you perceive in this excerpt?

How has Catherine the Great balanced rights with laws in this document? How did she define equality? In her view, what was the role of an enlightened monarch? What was the duty of each of her citizens? Are these ideas essentially liberal or conservative?

How does article 270 address Catherine's need to pacify the landed nobility of Russia? What were the consequences of her favoring this group?

Primary Sources on the French Revolution:

Declaration of the Rights of Man and Citizen

What similarities exist between this French document and the American Declaration of Independence? Why do such parallels exist?

Do yo perceive any further similarities between this Declaration of Rights and and American Bill of Rights? What specific rights and freedoms are protected in both?

Why was the American Bill of Rights attached to the Constitution, rather than to the Declaration of Independence?

Declaration of the Rights of Woman and the Female Citizen (1791)

Why did Olympe de Gouges assert that the Declaration of the Rights of Man and Citizen did not apply to women? How were women excluded from that original declaration?

According to the author, what rights were denied to eighteenth-century women? Was this only in France, or does she speak for all women?

What rights does the author argue should be granted to women? What positive results does she envision for freer women? For society as a whole?

What similarities do you perceive between the work of Olympe de Gouges in France and Mary Wollstonecraft in England? What effect did their writings have in eighteenth-century Europe? In their own countries?

Napoleon and Psychological Warfare: Proclamation to French Troops in Italy (April 26, 1796)

Who are "those arrogant kings" to whom Napoleon refers? Why did they oppose Napoleon's vision of Grand Empire?

When did Napoleon change his title from First Consul to Emperor Napoleon I? Why is might this be considered the end of the French Revolution?

VI. Artwork

Eighteenth-Century Art:

French Port of Dieppe

Who were France's chief competitors for trade in the New World? What were the results of such rivalries?

How did the concept of mercantilism shape European American trade and industry?

A Market in Turin

What were the differences and tensions between eighteenth-century town and country life? How did the vastly outnumbered urban dwellers maintain a measure of political power?

Why were the wealthy patrician urban elites not considered nobility? What qualified a person for membership in that "estate"? Was upward mobility between the estates possible?

The Death of Wolfe

Where were the two primary areas of conflict in the French and Indian War?

What factors enabled the British to win this war? Why did it start in the first place? Financially, how did Britain try to recover from the expenses incurred by defending the colonists? With what result?

Why did Spain add Florida to British territory after the Treaty of Paris?

Colonial Latin American Art:

Sor Juana Inés de la Cruz

In addition to convent, what other Catholic organizations were present in the Spanish-ruled Americas?

What new opportunities did the church provide for women?

Why would such a talented writer have been refused admission to the University of Mexico?

American Art:

The Declaration of Independence

What was accomplished by the First Continental Congress? By the second? Why was a second deemed necessary?

What issues drove the colonists to revolt against Britain? Was their revolt justified? Why did such issues, and general resentment of colonial rule, not lead to successful eighteenth-century revolts throughout the Americas?

Russian Art:

Catherine the Great

Consider this royal portrait alongside the previous portrait of Louis XIV in Chapter Fifteen. Why was presentation of self and court such a priority for absolutist rulers? Did "enlightenment" change such preoccupations?

Why is it especially appropriate for Catherine the Great to be presented in this fashion in the Temple of Justice? What legislative efforts did she make to improve Russia? Which classes were most affected?

What enlightened measures did Catherine the Great, Frederick the Great, and Joseph II pursue? How were their reforms limited?

Art of the French Revolution:

Storming of the Bastille

What was the Great Fear? How did the popular uprisings, such as the one depicted in this painting, contribute to this national crisis?

Why did French commoners storm the Bastille? Why was this attack more a symbolic act than a real achievement against an oppressive government?

Citizens Enlist in the New French Army

How did the original anti-French European coalition spur on French nationalism? Why were three such coalitions formed?

How did nationalism later aid Napoleon in France? How did its spread throughout Europe backfire on his wider ambitions for the Grand Empire?

Why do some scholars refer to the French Revolution as the first true "people's war"? What effect has this pattern had on modern warfare?

Women Patriots

To which of the three estates would the women pictured here most likely belong? How might their estate and financial standing influence their views on the National Convention decrees they are reading?

Are the women pictured here literate or illiterate? What effect would women's education have on their involvement with the Revolution?

Did women hold positions of leadership in the French revolution? What roles were assigned to them?

The Coronation of Napoleon

Why is it aptly said that Napoleon both destroyed and preserved aspects of the French Revolution?

Why did Napoleon restore monarchy in France rather than maintain a "people's republic"? Were his own ambitions or the welfare of France paramount in his decision?

What about David's painting strikes you as Absolutist in its representation of Napoleon and Josephine?

Why are Catholic clergy prominent in the painting? Given their presence, why does Napoleon, not the pope, place the crown on Josephine's head?

VII. Identifying Important Concepts Behind the Conclusion

The Conclusion to this chapter recalls the following key ideas:

1. Eighteenth-Century Europe: economic, social, military, and political systems, including "enlightened absolutism"

2. South and North American colonial systems, and colonial resistance: the American Revolution

3. French Revolution and the Age of Napoleon

Review these general concepts, and read the Reflection that follows this chapter, "The Emergence of New World Patterns (1500-1800)," before moving on to the next chapter.